WIN
THAT JOB

First edition copyright © Paul Lyons, 2010

www.paullyons.com

All rights reserved. No part of this book may be reproduced or transmitted in any form by any means, electronic or mechanical, including photocopying, recording or by any information storage or retrieval system, without prior permission in writing from the publisher. The Australian Copyright Act 1968 (the Act) allows a maximum of one chapter or 10 per cent of the book, whichever is the greater, to be photocopied by any educational institution for its educational purposes provided that the educational institution (or body that administers it) has given a remuneration notice to Copyright Agency Limited (CAL) under the Act.

A CIP catalogue of this book is available from the National Library of Australia

ISBN: 978-0-9807183-0-0 (pbk)

Edited by Joanna Tovia
Designed by Sharyn Raggett
Printed in China by Messenger Print Brokerage
Project managed by Messenger Publishing

www.messengerpublishing.com.au

WIN THAT JOB

PAUL LYONS

THE EXPERT'S ADVICE ON:
→ personal branding
→ career management
→ effective job search techniques

About this book and how to use it

This book will help you develop your personal brand, plan and manage your career and conduct an effective job search. You can use it as a comprehensive guidebook or just an aide for some specific practical advice. There are three sections – Career Management, Personal Branding and Job Search – each containing chapters on the key issues that you will face during your job search and career management process.

Contents

Part A: Successfully plan and manage your career

CHAPTER ONE — 13
The importance of career planning and management
Why planning and managing your career is essential	14
The process of career planning and management	16
Where are you now?	17
Where do you want to go?	18
How will you get there?	20
Ten smart career principles	21

CHAPTER TWO — 30
Understanding the employment market
Why the economy and the employment market are important to you as a job seeker	31
The health of the employment market influences employers' hiring styles	33
How the economy and employment market influence your career and job search strategies	34
Key trends to look for and where to find them	35
Working internationally	36

Part B: Brand yourself for success

CHAPTER THREE — 38
Where are you now? Building the 'You' brand
The importance of knowing yourself	39
You are unique	41
Undertake a personality profile	41
What is your personal brand and why is it important?	41
How to create your personal brand	42
Other factors to help you create and maintain	

your brand	43
How do you market your personal brand – what marketing collateral does it need?	44
Using your brand in your job search	48

Part C: Win that job – effective job search techniques

CHAPTER FOUR — 52
Overcoming common employment hurdles

Redundancy – fighting back	53
Other common hurdles – burnout and stress, boredom and career plateau, mid-life crisis, loss of self-esteem and confidence, recognition of wrong career path	55

CHAPTER FIVE — 59
Moving internally

Why internal opportunities are important	60
Being as good as you can be	62
Make your performance appraisals your scorecard	66
Negotiating a pay rise	67
Reasons to leave	69

CHAPTER SIX — 72
Moving externally – application letters and résumés that work

What is a résumé or CV?	73
The objective of application letters and résumés	73
Application letters that work	73
How to prepare a great résumé	74
Other important notes	77
What to leave out	78
Overcoming bad news in your résumé	79
Making your résumé stand out	82
Multi-media résumés	83
Update your résumé regularly	84
Ten don'ts on résumés	84

CHAPTER SEVEN — 87
The job search begins – where to look

Fifteen steps to a strong job search campaign	88
Respond to newspaper classified advertising	101
Surf the internet job sites and place your résumé online	101
Use your network	102
Use your brand – social and business networking sites	106
Approach employment agencies and executive recruiters	106
Target private sector employers	110
Approach government departments and agencies	112
Attend job fairs	112
Consider the contracting and interim option	113
Work for free	113
Working internationally and the importance of visas	114
What if your campaign isn't working?	115

CHAPTER EIGHT — 116
Facing the interview – prepare and perform

Understand how the interview works	117
Prepare yourself	120
Perform in the interview	124
The first five minutes	125
Answering difficult questions	126
Asking difficult questions	132
Finish in style	136
Video conference interviews	137
Follow up after the interview	137

CHAPTER NINE 139
Other selection criteria
Résumé review and portal applications	140
Psychometric tests	140
Reference checking	142
Social events	143
Security clearances	144

CHAPTER TEN 145
Common job search issues and solutions
Unsure of your next move?	146
Not winning interviews?	147
Finishing second in interviews	148
When there are too few opportunities	148
What to do if you are offered too low a salary	149
If your campaign isn't working	149

CHAPTER ELEVEN 151
Is it the job for you?
Analyse the job in relation to your plan	152
Negotiate to make it attractive	154
Decline with dignity	156
Resigning and dealing with counter offers	156
Depart professionally	159

CHAPTER TWELVE 160
Make the best start to your new job
Prepare to succeed	161
Week one – create a favourable impression	162
Month one – focus on relationships and productivity	163
Your first three months – learn to understand the culture	164
After three months – build your profile and performance	165

Part A

Successfully plan and manage your career

Chapter one

The importance of career planning and management

Why planning and managing your career is essential

At the beginning of your career you have access to a myriad of career choices – what degree to study at university, which occupation or profession to pursue and, broadly, what kind of employer you wish to work for.

With these choices comes responsibility – responsibility for your own destiny and for the direction in your career and your life. It is now you the individual that must manage your career and make the decisions that guide you in one direction or another.

Actively planning and managing your career will substantially increase your chances of short- and long-term career satisfaction and success.

We live in an era of constant change. The economy and employment market place is very different to that of five years ago and will be very different again in five years' time. The opportunities then will be different to those now and your challenge is to ensure that you are as marketable in five years as you are now.

Be aware that such changes will affect you positively, with opportunities that you never thought possible, or negatively, through the loss of your job due to a restructuring or company takeover, the loss of a major order or client, or the appointment of a new manager who doesn't like your style. There are no guarantees of employment anymore.

You need to know at any point in time the quality of your skills and experience and their relevance and value in the marketplace. You need to ensure that if your job disappears tomorrow your career can continue to progress and flourish because you are in demand by other employers.

If you fail to accumulate a collection of marketable skills and experience and you lose your job, your career will most likely stall because you either remain unemployed or are underemployed.

Similarly, you need to plan and manage for the future.

Your career links a series of jobs like a thread through your life into a discernable and potentially valuable pattern. To be successful in your career you should have a vision of where you want to go, not only medium/long-term but short-term too, and have a plan on how to get there. By planning systematically the steps you need to take – and the jobs you need to take and succeed in – you substantially increase your chances of getting to where you want to go in a career sense and being happy and fulfilled along the way.

If you don't plan or manage your career, it doesn't mean you won't be successful – it just dramatically reduces the likelihood of you being so because you are leaving your career to chance and other influences. The saying 'If you fail to plan, you plan to fail' is very relevant here.

Having a career plan in place is also important as a reference point for assessing opportunities. During your career you will likely be presented with unexpected job or promotion opportunities and assessing these opportunities against your plan can be an excellent way of assessing its quality and relevance. You are more likely to make the right decision for you with your plan in place.

A good analogy to career planning and management is being in a sailboat. To navigate safely and successfully you need to know yourself and your boat's capabilities. You need to know where you are setting out from and where you are headed to. You also need to be very aware of the weather and its likely impact on your journey.

Letting the winds and currents take you anywhere once you have begun your voyage is not only dangerous and life threatening but also very unlikely to take you to your destination. You set your course to your destination and then change your approach as different weather or tidal patterns become evident or as other shipping dictates. With good planning and management, and a little luck, you will reach your destination. So it is with your career planning and management

The process of career planning and management

Before you begin any journey – actual or metaphysical – there are three questions to be answered: Where are you now? (your starting point); Where do you want to go? (your destination); and How will you get there? (your route) and this is so with your career journey.

Once you reach mid-career, the years quickly slide by and it's easy to forget about your career and to 'freewheel', particularly when you have an acute shortage of time and are juggling family and work demands. You then find that you attend to your career only when you hit a crisis and often you are then doing so from a position of weakness rather than strength.

For that reason you should get in the habit at the beginning of your career of conducting your own Career Audit. Allocate one day each year in which you conduct a 'career check' and review your career plan. Ideally, pick a day at a similar time each year.

During this Career Audit you should review the following:

→ **Where are you now?**
Analyse your current career inventory – your knowledge, skills, experience and personal attributes. Conduct the self-analysis exercises in Chapter Three to help update your thoughts.

→ **Where do you want to go?**
Review your short- and medium-term career goals and ensure

you are in the right position to obtain skills and experience that can help you achieve those goals.

→ **How will you get there?**
Will your current position provide you with the knowledge, skills and experience and, ultimately, the opportunity to get you into your desired position either immediately or over a defined period of time? If you're not in the right position then you have to take action in some way to get in the right position.

None of this analysis can be completed in isolation from the job market. What are the trends in the demand and supply of skills in the job market? If they are changing, how do they affect you now and your future career goals?

Career planning and management is a simple concept although you can make it as comprehensive and sophisticated as you want. It is your strategic plan to make you successful.

This is not a scientific or even precise methodology but it will help guide you. Certainly write your plan down using the three simple headings (Where am I now?, Where do I want to go? and How will I get there?). Also, keep all your career plans and work information such as performance appraisals, job specifications and your résumé in one place for easy access and reference. It can be extremely useful to be able to access your job description of three years ago if you need to build a résumé for a specific job application.

Managing your career successfully enables you to achieve forward momentum in your work life and this will help you achieve career success.

Where are you now?

This is your starting point for the rest of your career and, whether you plan to move internally or externally, 'Where you are now' will have an impact on the move you will be able to make.

Analyse your career to date and why and how you are in your current position. You need to know, and certainly potential employers will be interested to know, why you have made the decisions you have made to get you into your current position. Employers will prefer to see logical reasons for the moves you have made.

Analyse yourself. As discussed above, it's vitally important to understand who you are, the nature of your strengths and preferences, visions and values, and where you are in your life and your career.

If you are early in your career, your starting point (Where are you now?) is important but has far less impact on your next job and future career than if you are mid- or mature-career when it becomes a critical factor in job moves and plans.

Where do you want to go?

'If you don't know where you are going, you'll never get there.'

As the above saying rightly suggests, having a clearly defined career goal is an essential part of you achieving career success. It's a statement to you and others about being in control of your destiny and direction.

A simple exercise to assist you in setting your goals is to write them down. Commit to paper what you want to have achieved in your career in one year, three years, five years and 15 years. These goals are likely to be more specific and achievable the closer they are to the present time. Ideally, there should be a consistent pattern between the four reference points so that the one-year goals lead into the three-year goals and so on. It's important to date your record for future reference and perhaps make the one-year goal, in particular, visible to you on a daily basis. Putting your goal on the fridge or on your mobile phone can be a positive motivator to you achieving your goals.

There are several important considerations to setting your career goals:

Defining what career success means to you
Defining and measuring your career success is an important component in crystallising your career goals. How will you assess, to yourself most importantly but those around you as well, whether you have been successful at the end of your career and along the way? This may be through job satisfaction, salary, status and so on. You also have to be vigilant as your thoughts on this may change over the course of your career meaning you have to redefine your goals to account for these changes.

Planning with a lack of clarity
In the early stages of your career it can be difficult to focus on a clear vision because you have so many choices and the end of your career seems so far in the future. You tend to focus on role models – people you know – and titles as well as financial goals. As you move through the mid- and mature-career stages, your goals tend to become pragmatic and have a much shorter timeframe.

In search of a passion
Focusing on short-term and long-term goals that excite you and will enable you to make best use of your talents will increase your chances of performing at a higher level and achieving your career goals. For that reason it's always good to dream a little and not instantly dismiss that voice inside your head that's encouraging you to reach for a seemingly improbable target.

Setting goals leads to discarding other goals
Sometimes people avoid setting goals because it means consciously ruling out other goals that are mutually exclusive – this can be disappointing. Although achieving one goal does often prevent achieving another, the real danger is that without any goal setting you substantially increase the chances of not achieving any goals at all.

Goals change over time
Like life goals, career goals change over time as your experiences alter your views and dreams. While this is natural, it's better that they evolve rather than change radically because a radical change in your goals can require you to make radical changes to your life and career. The more radical this change, the more likely you will experience a dislocation to your present and immediate future circumstances.

Your career goals should be achievable
While it is healthy to dream about your long-term future, you do need to have short- and medium-term goals that are realistic and achievable. This is important because you want to move your career ahead in small steps so that you give yourself at least a chance of achieving your long-term goals. Also, the feeling of forward momentum and achievement is a huge motivator to you setting more career goals and so continuing the process. If you don't achieve your goals one year, then by definition your career has most likely stopped progressing and that's a situation you want to avoid.

How will you get there?

This question is the final part of the career plan trilogy and is the link to the other two. It's the most practical component of your career plan and impacts directly on your job search. You want to identify the stepping stones that will get you from where you are now to where you want to go – and especially where you want to be in a year's time:

→ What are the skills you need to develop, attitudes you should adopt and experience you have yet to gain?

→ Do you need to undertake further education or attend professional development courses?

→ Do you need to expand your responsibilities at work and can you learn enough from your manager or do you need to find another job that will enable you to do so?

→ Are you in the right industry sector and are your plans achievable in the current climate?

Again, the process is best committed to paper. Write down the process of getting to where you want to be in a year's time. This is your 'to do' list.

It may include an internal move or external move and, if it does, the following chapters will be important for you.

Ten smart career principles

In this world of uncertainty, navigating your way through the stormy job market can be challenging. As discussed above, there are few certainties attached to decisions made by you or your employer and more than ever it is important for you to take control of managing your career to reduce the risks of becoming obsolete.

Here are 10 smart career principles to help you plan and manage your career:

1. Take responsibility for managing your career. You own your career – your employer owns your job.

It's essential that you take responsibility for managing your own career. Regrettably, most people spend more time researching and organising their annual vacation than they do analysing and managing their career. Few people actively and logically plan and manage their career in the manner required to achieve career success.

Most people tend to be passive about their career, only actively considering issues when they meet an opportunity or face a hurdle. One of the key issues in career management is that you own your career and your employer owns your job. Your career has permanence and is always with you – your job is only temporary and your job and its owner – your employer – can change many times over the life of your career.

While in most cases your career and job are closely aligned, when you begin your job they become less congruent over time as either your goals and aspirations and the skills and experience required to achieve those goals change or your employer wishes to make changes to the nature of the role.

So you and you alone are responsible for ensuring that you are developing the right skills and experience and that your career is moving in the right direction.

Similarly it is your employer's responsibility to ensure that the job you have contributes to the organisation. It's not their responsibility to ensure that it changes and develops so you can broaden your skills and experience and advance your career. While some organisations do assume this responsibility, there is absolutely no legal, commercial or moral requirement for them to do so.

2. When you are young, you 'sell' your potential to employers. As you get older you convert that potential into skills and experience and 'sell' your track record.

As a young person, you leave school or university with (hopefully) a school certificate or degree, technical, professional or academic qualifications and then seek a first job to begin your career. At this stage you have both your life and career ahead of you and you have the potential to be anyone and attain any position there is.

Unfortunately, this is purely a temporary phenomenon and as the months and years progress you start to convert this potential into experience and a track record. In your first job you gain knowledge, skills and experience, you begin to enhance your social and communication skills and develop your attitudes to work. Depending on your relative success in this role, you then move onto a better job with your existing employer and then onto another and another. In no time at all you are either 'fulfilling' and 'realising' your potential by developing a valuable profile that is in demand or you are establishing a less impressive track record that will lead you to a lower trajectory career path.

It is important for you to know that from day one you are converting potential to experience which in turn forms your track record. While you can enhance or extend your potential by overachieving, it is just as likely that you will reduce your potential by underachieving.

3. The older and more experienced you become, the harder it becomes to find a job that will progress your career.

Strangely, the older one gets the harder it becomes to find a job and certainly one that will progress your career. As you enter your thirties and forties, you develop a far greater array of knowledge, skills and experience and have a much greater insight into your occupation or profession thereby being able to increasingly add value to your employer. However, the number of opportunities open to you as an older executive falls dramatically due to the pyramid hierarchy effect of fewer senior management or technical positions being available as you become more senior. The progressive flattening of corporate structures over the past 10 years has made this problem worse.

At the same time the competition for those jobs increases, as there are many more eligible applicants in their thirties, forties and fifties.

In contrast, as a younger person you possess more limited skills and experience but find it relatively easy to find a job because there are many junior jobs and fewer or a similar number of job seekers to fill those jobs.

4. You will be accountable for every decision you make about your career.

As you convert your potential into experience you will realise that you become acutely accountable for every career decision and move that you make. Decisions that you made on the spur of the moment 10 years previously can come back to haunt you. In the cold light of day and in different circumstances, they sometimes appear naïve and ill informed.

This doesn't mean that you shouldn't take risks or that it's career suicide to make mistakes (it definitely isn't) but it does mean that you will need to be able to discuss and justify why you made the career decisions you did. For example, in the current economic climate, job seekers who made many moves earlier in their career chasing the mighty dollar at the expense of building their résumé are now finding that potential employers are focusing keenly on values and stability and so are critical of those moves.

5. Always aim to achieve forward momentum in your career.

Career management is anything but an exact science. There are no qualifications that guarantee you a successful career and few failsafe reference points that can determine you are developing a successful career. Status and salary are obviously two indicators but they can be temporary and aren't always a true reflection of your career success.

Job satisfaction is vitally important but probably the best is the sense of forward momentum in your career – that you are developing skills and experiences that will equip you better to face the challenges ahead. Of course it's a subjective measure but generally, forward momentum is a sign of a career that's healthy.

Once you feel that you have stopped progressing and that you are no longer being stretched or challenged at work (often described as a rut or plateau) your career is in danger.

6. Always aim to develop experience that is marketable.

You convert your potential into experience as you move from entry level through to mature-career stage. Potential here is defined as your potential to perform to the required level and then to continue to grow in the future to perform at higher levels.

In the early stages you sell yourself internally and externally largely on potential. Moving through your career you then sell a combination of potential and experience and then onto the mature-career stage where it is predominately your track record of experience that you are selling.

The experience you gain is obviously significant as it will sell you or not sell you in your career. There are some important observations:

→ You should always plan to gain experience that will be a stepping stone in the career direction you want to go.

→ If you are unclear as to your precise career goal then try to develop experience that will help you keep your options open.

→ In the early stages of your career, try different things not only to find out what you like but what you're good at. You won't often get the opportunity to do so later in your career as such a move will be perceived as being 'unstable'.

→ In the early part of your career, aim to achieve a combination of solid, 'middle-of-the-road' experience in your particular discipline but then also other 'out of the ordinary' experience that stretches you in a different direction such as ad hoc

→ projects or difficult or stressful situations. In this way you gain both the required basic experience and attractive additional experience which makes you much more marketable internally and externally.

→ There should always be a logical thread running through your experience so the different positions that comprise your experience to date read logically like a book, each position leading naturally into the next. Your experience should not only be relevant to your longer term career goals and leading you in the general direction of where you want to go but also needs to be relevant short term to ensure you are marketable for the next opportunity.

→ Future employers will look at your résumé for relevant company labels and position labels and, depending on their own credentials and preferences, will prefer certain labels and combinations of labels. For example, a large company will usually be more interested in someone with prior large company experience. This does vary during the economic cycle but certainly in a downturn it is much more likely that an employer will want to see experience as close as possible to the vacant position and from a company of a similar size, style and structure.

→ Employers look for evidence of promotions and lateral moves within one company because it proves you have talents and qualities that have been recognised and rewarded. *[margin note: This is a strong selling point ←]*

→ Your experience will be both the cause and effect of a successful or mediocre career.

7. Know when to take career risks and when to consolidate.

In order to be successful in your career, you will have to take risks. You will face barren times with seemingly no opportunities to push out the boundaries and other times where you have too many options. Having your career plan in place will help you to analyse what you need to make happen or, alternatively, the relevance of opportunities that are presented to you. It's important to understand your risk profile – essentially how much job security you are prepared to risk in order to achieve a position that better satisfies your career goals. Often it can be harder to take career risks when you have a secure, well-paid job than when you don't since what you have to lose is greater but sometimes that security can be the constraint to your career progress.

Another important factor is the health of the economy and the job market in your sector. It is generally better to consolidate in a tough economic climate and stay put in your existing job since alternative jobs are more difficult to come by – and then take risks in the good times when there are more opportunities. However this again depends on your own circumstances and risk profile.

8. Your soft skills and personal characteristics are an important ingredient in your career success.

Soft skills and particularly your communication skills – verbal, written, social and listening – as well as key personal traits such as trust and integrity are important ingredients if you wish to become a successful manager and leader.

Developing these skills and traits allows you to progress from transactional or specialist technical roles to positions with broader people and project management responsibilities.

If you have strong social skills you will be rewarded with supervisory responsibilities which, if you perform successfully, will be the first steps to a successful career in management. You will be promoted because people believe you can manage a situation and/or a group of people successfully and without fuss.

Certainly at the senior levels of an organisation people are hired or appointed on the basis of trust and their ability to make an impact on the business.

While your personal characteristics are inherent by the time you reach the workforce, you certainly can and should practise your soft skills because they are very much on show during the job search process. Demonstrating good social skills will set you apart from most of your competitors.

9. Training and re-skilling should be a lifetime practice.
It's no longer enough to be educated and trained at the entry point to your career and then rely on your experience to get you through your career unscathed. With the economy changing so quickly, demand for certain skills and experience can appear and disappear within a matter of years, particularly in the technology field. It's therefore vital that as part of your career plan you also take responsibility for staying up to date with the latest trends and techniques not only in your chosen occupation or profession but also those in technology, which will impact on your day-to-day work.

While many good employers will help you in this by ensuring that you attend training courses relevant to your current job or organisation, you need to be aware of the additional qualifications and skills required to get you the next job and the one after that which will enable you to achieve career progression.

A good guide is to pick at least one skill every year that you need to update or acquire. Certainly a key asset is a second degree sometime mid-career that will update your conceptual framework. It obviously needs to relate to your current and future career path and is important not only for the value it adds to your day-to-day work but also the perception from employers that you are serious about your career.

10. It's better to be 'employable' than 'employed'.
Your focus should be on being employable rather than being employed. Being employed can be a temporary status. If you lose your job for whatever reason then you may or may not get another one depending on your skills, experience and the job market. If you focus on being employable you will always retain

the skills and experience that are marketable and in demand and therefore you are far less likely to be out of work for long should you lose your current job.

> **TAKE ACTION**
> 1. Do a Career Audit to assess where you are now, where you want to go and the steps you will need to take to get there.
>
> 2. Don't rely on your employer to dictate your next move. Move your career forward by developing the right skills and experience to make you marketable and in demand.

Chapter two

Understanding the employment market

Why the economy and the employment market are important to you as a job seeker

The local, regional and global economies change from good to bad and back again and the changing economies will affect you and your career as the health of those economies determine the employment market.

Everyone in work or wanting to be in work needs to be an 'active observer' of the economy and its impact on the employment market. The local regional and world economies change constantly and while in some years these changes are negligible, in other years they can be dramatic. These changes can in turn significantly alter the characteristics of the job market and your chances of finding the job you want.

Each economy experiences cyclical and structural changes on a regular basis. The cyclical changes occur as each market-based economy ebbs and flows causing a weak economy to grow stronger over time and then 'overheat' and become weaker again.

These changes directly affect employment. In a weak and declining economy, more organisations rationalise, close or merge causing jobs to be lost. In a strong, growing economy more jobs are created as organisations in the private and public sectors grow, new companies are established and fewer jobs disappear through closure or merger.

These positive cycles usually last 7–10 years before a decline although the last one was approximately 15 years, albeit with some dips along the way.

Each economy also has structural issues that affect employment and these are usually determined by government policy on tariffs and subsidies, by a significant event or economic situation or by population patterns.

Whilst the economy will usually affect employment in line with the trend, that's not always the case as different economic cycles and structural issues will affect different industries and companies in different ways. Even in a weak economy, some companies and industry sectors perform well and recruit more people while in a strong economy some industries and individual organisations suffer and jobs are lost.

The laws of supply and demand dictate the employment market and who has control of the market.

In a strong economy and therefore strong employment market, demand for labour rises, creating more job vacancies and more jobs. As those jobs are taken up, the supply of available people falls and in time a shortage of people in that particular sector or occupation occurs. As a result, organisations begin to compete for employees by offering better salaries and employment benefits and focusing on creating better, longer term career opportunities to attract and retain staff.

This becomes an employees' market, where if you have the right skills and experience you can have the choice of many well-paid career opportunities with prominent organisations.

Conversely, in a weak economy and therefore weak employment market demand for labour falls, reducing both the volume of jobs and job vacancies. It also increases the supply of available people and in time a shortage of jobs in that particular sector or occupation occurs. As a result salaries begin to fall as individuals begin to compete for employers by working longer hours for lower salaries and fewer benefits. This becomes an employers' market where employers can reduce their payroll costs, employ fewer, better people and increase their productivity.

The health of the employment market influences employers' hiring styles

Not only are employers inclined to hire fewer people as their business declines or more people as it improves but the nature of their recruitment also changes.

In a weak economy with tougher operating conditions, their profit margins are squeezed and they become much more focused on their immediate survival than their medium- to long-term growth.

Employers become more risk averse and seek to hire individuals that immediately understand the organisation's issues, who need limited induction time, can create an immediate positive impact and who quickly add value. Since employers have little margin for error they can less afford to hire someone that may not fit in or contribute straight away.

This affects you, as the employee or prospective employee, in two ways.

Firstly, employers become more specific about the skills, experience and personal qualities they are seeking. They tend to focus heavily on the relevance of your track record of experience and particularly the most recent experience to the job in hand and less about your potential to contribute in the long term. The closer the fit, the more likely you are to be considered.

This makes it more difficult for people without relevant experience (entry-level trainees, career changers, immigrants) or those with career hurdles such as unemployment or unusual experience to find appropriate positions.

Secondly, employers also become much more stringent in the hiring process and probably won't appoint you unless they are absolutely sure you are the right fit for the role. The selection process is likely to involve more interviews and reference checks and possibly aptitude testing so you need to prepare more thoroughly, perform better than your contemporaries and be patient throughout the process.

Not only do employers want to be specific in their hiring, they can afford to be because the supply of available candidates means they have many people to choose from.

In a better economy, the emphasis and style is different.

Employers are more confident about the short-term success of their business and so focus on building for the future. They look to hire people who don't necessarily possess precise relevant recent experience but who do have the skills and the potential to contribute in the future years.

They also have to be more flexible in their desired profiles because it's a much more competitive job market and there are fewer people available with the right experience.

How the economy and employment market influence your career and job search strategies

Whether you are a graduate seeking your first job, a chief executive or somewhere in between, the economy and employment market will influence your career and job search strategies.

Not only do cyclical trends and structural issues in the economy affect the employment market and the demand for your services but there are also trends, issues and opportunities within your occupation or industry sector that change over time the skills and experience in demand.

To stay relevant and employable and to pursue these opportunities you need to be able to anticipate and recognise these trends and then develop the necessary skills and experience.

Whether seeking a role internally or externally you need to be an 'active observer' of the economy and employment market.

Key trends to look for and where to find them

In being an active observer you need to be aware of the impact of the following on your job and career:

→ The current and likely future state of the local regional and world economies

→ The development of any significant structural local or regional issues or events

→ Any government initiatives or changes to policy

→ Specific trends and issues that could impact on your occupation and industry sector

→ Local news relating to employment such as the unemployment rate and any company announcements on hiring or layoffs

→ News of your own organisation's trading and market performance locally and, if applicable, globally.

This information isn't always easy to find but to stay informed you should:

→ Read a daily newspaper regularly with particular emphasis on the business and financial markets news

→ Read at least one professional or trade journal relevant to your occupation. These are usually published monthly

→ Access the websites of relevant recruitment companies and job boards for information on market trends and hot skills, particularly those in your sector. If you are not actively looking for a job this doesn't need to be more than three or four times a year.

Working internationally

All of the above considerations apply to working internationally but additional research is required because you are researching a new lifestyle as well as a new career. In addition to researching business customs and demands, you need to research the availability and cost of working visas, accommodation and, if you have children, schools and support networks, requirement for languages and so on.

> **TAKE ACTION**
> 1. Become an active observer of the economy and its impact on the employment market to allow you to make educated career decisions.
>
> 2. Stay abreast of trends affecting your industry and occupation.

Part B

Brand yourself for success

Chapter three

Where are you now? Building the 'You' brand

The importance of knowing yourself

Although the health of the economy and the job market will influence your job search and your career, by far and away the biggest influence on your personal and career success and your success in finding a job will be you.

You largely determine your own success and by planning and managing your career effectively you can significantly improve your chances of being successful.

Rarely is the best qualified and most experienced person appointed to a job – it's usually the person who sells themselves the most effectively – internally or externally – through the job search process.

You are the best person by far to sell yourself in your job search or your career but to be able to take advantage of the opportunities and overcome the setbacks you need to know yourself inside out. The more you know about yourself the more likely you are to be able to sell yourself into a role and, more importantly, identify a career path that will make the most of your talents and provide you with lasting satisfaction and success.

This intense and thorough self-analysis can sometimes be difficult and confronting but it is the cornerstone to your career planning and management trilogy. Understanding where you are now provides you with a much better insight into deciding where you want to go (your goals, plans and dreams) and thus in turn to how you will get there (the career steps you must take).

We think you should build on your initial self-analysis to create the brand 'You' but even if you don't, at least complete the following simple exercises to better understand who you are and where you are in your career.

Firstly, write down your strengths (personal and work-related), preferences (what you enjoy doing most) and how you define success (personally and in your career). This could be with indicators such as financial rewards, job satisfaction, status, recognition and so on.

Then, similarly describe your development points or weaknesses (personal and work related) and dislikes (what you dislike doing most). Finally, define what failure would mean for you in your life and career. This exercise gives you a simple indicator of the person you are and want to be and the person you are not and wish not to be.

Secondly, identify the greatest accomplishments in your personal life and at work and your greatest setbacks. Describe in detail how those events made you feel.

Thirdly, using the self-analysis from the first two sections as well as other sources, write three words or phrases that you think describe you best (ambitious, organised and athletic, for example).

Ask people who know you well and perhaps some who don't know you so well to also write three words that describe you.

Compare the different perceptions of you with other people. Discuss with your referees and current and former colleagues and managers. Read through your performance management reviews for clues on who you are.

Hopefully the view of you by others will be the same as yours or, if not, that you are pleasantly surprised.

These basic exercises begin to help you understand who you are, what you are good at and enjoy doing and what is important to you in your career and your life.

They also help you in giving you positive words to write in your career profile or objective and to use when discussing your strengths with others. Being able to use positive action words will help you stand out from the crowd.

You are unique

You won't necessarily deduce this from your self-analysis but you (like everyone else in the workforce) are unique. Each person has a different background and pedigree, different experiences and abilities, different talents, different preferences and different personalities. You are different and you are unique and you need to identify and understand how. You will need to learn to identify what parts of your make-up are attractive to potential or existing employers and then learn to accentuate them.

Undertake a personality profile

A personality profile (sometimes called a psychological profile) can help you understand your personal behaviour and style profile. Usually contained within a series of questions lasting from a few minutes to the most advanced lasting most of one day, your answers to the questions posed of you will provide an insight into your likely behaviour in a range of given circumstances. The results are not a test giving right or wrong answers – they just portray the style of person you are and the traits you are likely to display.

It's well worth investing in a test such as Myers Briggs (one of the most comprehensive and widespread) as this is a useful reference tool to you and others and will form part of your brand image.

What is your personal brand and why is it important?

A personal brand is similar to a consumer brand. It is your identity and reputation, often highlighting signature strengths (and sometimes weaknesses). It's what makes you stand out from the crowd and be discussed and remembered in a positive, impactful way. It's the reputation you develop in your work through your manner and personality and through your values and attributes.

It's important because it's the way you are viewed and valued by others – customers, colleagues, managers and potential employers. If you have a positive brand, you enhance your chances of bigger and better opportunities. If your brand is broadly negative then you have big challenges in making the progress you want.

How to create your personal brand

Everyone can and should develop their 'uniqueness' into their brand so they stand out and are remembered and talked about in a positive way. Your challenge is to figure out how to distinguish yourself from your colleagues and contemporaries and to work out what it takes to create a distinctive role for yourself. You must create a message and strategy to promote the brand called 'You'.

Work with the results of your self-analysis (above) and personality profile. What characteristics do you want to be personally known for? What are words and phrases that come to mind that you can honestly use to describe yourself? For example, words which describe your traits and values might be trustworthy, creative or responsive. 'Accomplished media practitioner' would highlight your professional expertise.

If you use these words or phrases, they must fairly represent you and therefore be reaffirmed by people who know you and work with you and be able to be incorporated in your 'brand collateral' (referees' references, résumés, etc).

Finally, your brand should be consistent with where you want to go. By promoting and reinforcing your brand it should help you move your career in a direction to achieve your career and personal goals. If it won't, then you either are creating the wrong brand image and need to change it or have formulated the wrong goals and need to re-evaluate them.

Other factors to help you create and maintain your brand

You can reinforce your brand in other ways too. Invest in yourself through training or personal/professional development courses if you need to enhance a particular part of your brand.

It's also very important to achieve brand consistency to ensure that what you and others say about you is consistent via referrals and across blog sites, networking sites, video sites, web pages, message boards and forums.

A common mistake here is to portray two different people in the professional and personal domain. Clearly you can and should have different facets to you inside and outside work but they should portray a broadly consistent message. For example, being passionate about a sport or hobby can add to your brand image and help tell your story.

It is also helpful for internal career progression if your brand is aligned with your company values as those people making decisions about your career progression will value the alignment.

In the same way successful consumer brands are periodically reassessed, you should review your brand and your career progress – at least annually as part of your Career Audit – to keep it relevant. Your annual Career Audit gives you the opportunity to re-evaluate your strengths, preferences and values which change over time as well as your career goals and your plan for achieving them from here. The quieter time between Christmas and New Year is often a good time to conduct this.

Also ask colleagues, friends, peers, managers and recruiters for honest, helpful feedback on your performance, development and your value. It's the only way to know what you would be worth on the open market. It's the only way to make sure that, when you decide to move up or on, you'll be in a strong bargaining position.

How do you market your personal brand – what marketing collateral does it need?

To be effective, your brand image needs to be consistent in every way – through other people, communications such as application letters and résumés, and on personal and business networking websites such as Facebook and LinkedIn.

Everything you do and everything you choose not to do communicates the value and character of your brand. Everything from the way you handle phone conversations to the email messages you send to the way you conduct business in a meeting is part of the larger message you're sending about your brand.

The key to any personal branding campaign, however, is 'word-of-mouth marketing'. Your network of friends, referees, colleagues, clients and customers is the most important marketing tool you've got and what they say about you and your contributions is what the market will ultimately gauge as the value of your brand.

So the big first step in building your brand is to find ways to nurture your network of colleagues and contemporaries.

You influence how the people around you perceive you – you determine what you want them to see when they see you, meet with you and interact with you. These opinions are determined by the way you dress, the way you communicate with them, the way you project yourself personally and through your work. It is the quality of these opinions as well as the quality of your work that will determine your chances of internal career advancement.

It is particularly important that the decision makers in your company have a clear and positive understanding of what you do and that they like you and trust you to do a good job.

In creating and nurturing an internal network of people who have the power and influence to assist your progression within the organisation, you should specifically focus on these people:

Your direct manager

Ideally your direct manager should be your greatest supporter but this often isn't the case in practice. Nevertheless, you need to work hard to cultivate a good working relationship and the onus is on you to make it work. They ultimately have the final decision on your immediate future if they don't think the relationship is working well enough.

Clarify as soon as you can what performance level is expected of you and how your manager wants you to work. These guidelines are a useful framework for you but are also a useful indicator as to the style of your manager and the organisation. How comfortable and compatible you are with this style will ultimately be one of the factors that determines how long you stay with the organisation.

If your performance warrants it, your manager should be communicating your abilities to the management team so that you are considered for appropriate internal opportunities. But you can't rely on that happening. Some managers will know their own performance will be hampered by an effective subordinate moving on so will do their best to retain you in your current role for as long as possible.

You should be able to quickly form a picture of whether your manager is a supporter or suppressor by whether they take full credit for your (and other colleagues') work, their track record in doing so previously, the number of people who have left either internally (good) or externally (potentially bad) as well as their general 'style' (open or closed, formal or informal, for example).

Also use the power of association to your advantage. Assess your manager's ability and their 'place' within the organisation. If you, and others, rate your manager highly then try to develop a close professional relationship with them not only because you can learn from them at work but also because they may assist you in your career whether they stay at your current organisation or move on to take other external opportunities. They could become one of your referees and mentors.

If you don't 'rate' them, then you should remain courteous and professional but distance yourself from wholesale support and endorsement of their ideas and practices to avoid being 'tainted' by that association.

Your manager's manager
You're unlikely to be party to the quality of the relationship between your own manager and his/her manager and how your abilities are being communicated up the line. For this reason, be creative and make (and take) every opportunity to impress and be visible to your manager's manager.

You want to ensure that you form a positive impression that increases your own chances of progression if a suitable opportunity arises. Since this could be the only sighting of you and your work, you have to ensure they are impressed by what they see.

If you can't get access while your manager is present then you may have to wait until your manager is absent (vacation, illness, business trip, etc) but don't misuse the reporting lines or you could disenfranchise yourself from both individuals.

Other influential managers
Managers in the same function or other functions can also be useful supporters, particularly if they feel they can make better use of your talents and can offer you better opportunities. Demand for your services from more than one manager within your organisation will ensure you are discussed and noticed.

Meet these managers through working parties or cross-functional project teams that provide you with additional experience and exposure or through social events or training sessions.

Down by the water cooler

Within every organisation there are people who promote certain unofficial but nevertheless important views to anyone and everyone who will listen at the 'water cooler'. These are people who have been with the organisation for quite some time and seem to know what's going on and with whom, and if they don't know they will probably be able to make a good guess.

This ensures that information, factual and otherwise, is disseminated up, around and down the organisation. They are usually people in positions such as the Office Manager, Receptionist or the Security Manager that involve having access to a continual supply of official and unofficial information.

They are people you want to stay on the right side of because they can influence the view of you within the organisation and a friendly exchange every day can be a valuable investment.

Your colleagues

There will be people you like more than others within your working group but you should ensure that you are generally a popular member of staff or at least not an unpopular one. Your manager will hear feedback about you from the others (in the same way you will give feedback about them) and whether it's consistently positive, negative or mixed will have an impact on your manager's view of you and your career potential.

Human resources department

If your organisation is large enough it is likely to have a human resources department which will seek to ensure that talent within the organisation is recognised and promoted. Internal vacancies will usually be publicised on the company's intranet or staff notice board.

You should ensure that you establish a dialogue with the HR team responsible for your function and if possible arrange at least an annual meeting to discuss the company and the career opportunities that may be relevant to you.

Using your brand in your job search

If, after a thorough analysis of yourself, your achievements to date and your career goals, you have decided you need to obtain another job either within or outside your current organisation then you need to consider incorporating your 'brand' into your job search.

Securing or 'winning' a new job is much to do with self promotion – it's about convincing the hiring decision maker that you have the best package of skills and experience for the job. It's irrelevant whether or not you do, although of course the message you project should be accurate and legitimate and not fabricated for the purpose of the application.

Volvo cars have a reputation for safety when there are many cars that fulfill similar safety requirements. Similarly, Starbucks coffee retail outlets have become synonymous with coffee around the world even though there are other chains of shops that produce coffee to arguably a higher standard. It should be your goal to achieve similar brand recognition with potential employers.

If you have a clear idea of who you are and your strengths and goals then the message you communicate to potential employers is likely to be convincing and plausible.

If you haven't already done so, discuss your plans with your referees. Referees are often more experienced than you and work in a position of authority. They know you and can comment on your personality and workplace performance. Potential employers like to discuss who you are with your referees before making you a formal job offer. Referees can provide potential employers with information and comments about you that have some credence and authority.

Ideally these referees are previous managers of yours and so are ideally placed to comment without you incurring the risk of your employer knowing that you are looking for a job. You should ask their permission to be your referee before you commence your job search.

Referees will be a useful sounding board for you on your plans and will help you formulate your message to the job market.

It's important that you and your referees are promoting the same message to potential employers – any differences will detract from the strength of your message and the application itself.

Your list of 'three words' from your self-analysis earlier in the chapter will help you achieve clarity on who you are. Using these and other information from your self-analysis, you should also write a 10- to 15-word sentence that best describes who you are. This is your career commercial, your advertising slogan, which you will use in your job search, in résumés, applications, telephone scripts and interviews to describe the essence of you. Spend time on it to construct a slogan that you are happy to use. An example could be: 'Accomplished finance executive with substantial international resources sector experience, especially in the fields of strategy and M&A'. Another could be: 'Hardworking and enthusiastic marketing graduate with strong creative and business skills'.

One critical piece of advice in both defining your message and searching for your job is to 'be confident and act confident'. Hiring managers like confidence and look for confidence. Being confident will get you into places and situations that you wouldn't otherwise reach and being confident will get you more interviews and job offers than not being confident.

Finally, ensure that your Facebook, Bebo, LinkedIn and other networking site entries portray a consistent brand image ... or be prepared for unexpected questions about photographs or comments you would rather your potential employer did not see.

> **TAKE ACTION**
> 1. Do some thorough self-analysis using the methods outlined in this chapter. The more you know about yourself, the more likely you are to be able to sell yourself into a satisfying role.
>
> 2. Create an accurate brand image of yourself that will help you stand out from the crowd in a positive way.
>
> 3. Incorporate your brand into your job search to communicate who you are.

Part C

Win that job – effective job search techniques

Chapter four

Overcoming common employment hurdles

Redundancy – fighting back

Whatever the health of the economy, there is regrettably always unemployment among professionals and executives as their companies close or merge. Unemployment can be one of the most stressful and traumatic events in your life, particularly if you are mid-career and the news is unexpected.

However, sometimes it can also provide an excellent opportunity for you to break the mould and change direction to a more successful career. There are some important points to consider:

→ **It is your position, not you, that has become redundant.**
Unless you are being made redundant for a lack of performance or for transgressing the terms of your contract, the reason for your dismissal will be because your role no longer exists, not because you are redundant. This may not make you feel any better but it should.

→ **It's acceptable to feel aggrieved.**
When it first happens you may feel a range of emotions, especially anger but also relief, uncertainty, betrayal, bitterness and sadness. These are all justifiable and normal. You should spend time coming to terms with the decision and getting the emotion out of your system as much as you can. You shouldn't under any circumstances start to look for another job until you've come to terms with your redundancy as your anger and bitterness will be evident during the selection process and will deter potential employers. If you can't shake your loss after 4-5 weeks, then you may need to seek guidance from professional counsellors to help you through this stage.

→ **Exit with dignity.**
However tempting it may be to express your real feelings during the exit process, try to harness your anger and exit professionally and with dignity. You will need the help of your former colleagues and managers in the coming months for references and contacts.

→ **Obtain your entitlements.**
Also ensure that you receive from your former employer any financial or other assistance (eg. outplacement programs) you are entitled to. If you are uncertain of the process, contact an employment lawyer to ensure that you have received all your entitlements and that your redundancy has been handled in the right way. While expensive, this process can also help your healing process as it quickly focuses your mind on what has happened and what you have to do.

→ **Communicate with your family and your friends.**
Don't hide your redundancy. Since it will have an enormous impact on the lives of your family it's important that you explain what has happened and that there may be some changes ahead. Similarly, tell your closest friends although it's probably best not to make this a general broadcast until you have a plan and can ask for specific help generating leads.

→ **Construct a financial plan.**
One of your immediate issues will be financial. Whether or not you have received severance pay or bonuses, you should undertake a thorough review of your budget for the year ahead. Ensure that you have received all your entitlements from the organisation and that your pension payments are in order. Register for any government benefits you may be entitled to. Reduce all non-essential expenditure and assume that your new budget will need to last a full year until you are back on your feet again.

→ **Undergo the self-review process.**
Once you feel reconciled to what has happened, it's time to move on and to think about the future. You certainly need to undergo the self-review process outlined in Chapter Three and plan a strategy for the next stage in your career.

→ **Know how to explain your termination to potential employers.**
Discuss your termination and the reasons for it with your

employer and your other referees. There is regrettably still a stigma attached to being unemployed and some potential employers may think your departure is performance related until you can convince them otherwise. Therefore it's important that you understand the reasons for your termination, that you can communicate this with confidence to the market and that your referees, including your former employer, can back this up verbally and in writing. You need to ensure that there is no doubt whatsoever surrounding the reasons for your departure otherwise this could harm your job search.

→ **Set yourself a realistic time frame for finding a new role.**
Be prepared that it could take several months to find the right job – more if you are seeking a specialist or senior position or if you don't have the requisite skills or experience.

→ **Be persistent and positive during your job search.**
Always ensure that you remain professional, positive and persistent during your job search.

Other common hurdles

It is common in your career to experience hurdles that sour your job satisfaction and confidence and threaten to derail your career progression. Although unemployment can have the most significant and lasting effect, each hurdle needs to be identified and tackled before it harms your progress.

Below are some of the common hurdles and some suggestions for overcoming them:

Burnout and stress
Workplace stress is becoming more widespread as more people work increasingly long hours under pressurised conditions. While acceptable for short periods of time, burnout and stress can certainly impair your health and emotional wellbeing and derail

your career if allowed to continue for months and years.

While you invariably need a single-minded focus to reach the top, it certainly helps you get there and stay there if you are well rounded with broad interests and social skills.

You will experience stress as the different parts of your life clash for time and then, if work remains number one, you will lose your balance with the other parts of your life (family, friends, leisure), which will then fade away and leave an even greater dependence on work. It becomes a vicious cycle.

Tackle it through these three steps:

→ Acknowledge that the situation must change to prevent doing harm to yourself and your career.

→ Try to compartmentalise your job and then look to delegate or remove the non-essential components.

→ Rediscover other important parts of your life as a balance and block out days/times in your diary to ensure that work doesn't encroach.

Boredom and career plateau

Although not as debilitating personally, boredom and career plateau can still be a career stopper. Your work has stopped motivating you and you have little or no job satisfaction or fresh challenges. It is likely that you have stopped using your full range of skills and abilities and certainly you have no sense of forward momentum or learning.

There may also be signs that you are out of favour and that your influence is waning and progression threatened. There may be no recent signs that you are making progress or colleagues less experienced or able than yourself may be winning promotion or selection on projects ahead of you.

The solution is again in your hands. If you are sure of your skills and career goals, then analyse your job and look to add more responsibilities, increase the standards of service you are providing and set new goals. If none of these can get your career moving again internally, then perhaps you need to look outside your organisation.

Mid-life crisis
A personal crisis can happen any time but it's often more prevalent in mid-career as you realise that your early dreams are not coming together and you haven't made the progress you would have liked in your life and career.

You are increasingly impatient and frustrated with those around you and you think you're not getting the feedback or recognition you deserve. The grass is definitely greener on the other side.

The solution here is to avoid making any sudden moves or acting on impulse. Instead, carefully and objectively assess your life and career and then plan to vary your lifestyle or work.

Loss of self-esteem and confidence
Losing your self-esteem and confidence can often happen after a period of poor performance or not working and the key is to focus on achieving sustained self improvement – lots of little steps and 'wins' that alone may appear to lack substance but which together can get your confidence, and career, moving in the right direction again.

Recognition of wrong career path
Many people fall into the wrong career often through chance or peer/parental pressure. Sometimes it is difficult to recognise but symptoms are a sustained lack of satisfaction and success in your job while feeling confident that the best of you is yet to come. What you need is a serious career self-analysis and to research alternative career options with a view to building a bridge between your current skills and abilities and those required in your choice of future career.

TAKE ACTION
1. If redundancy strikes, allow yourself some time then use it to your advantage.

2. Don't accept burnout and stress as your lot in life – actively work on creating a more balanced existence.

3. If your job is far from satisfying, make changes to your job or start looking for a new one.

Chapter five

Moving internally

Why internal opportunities are important

Developing your career within your current organisation can be one of the best career decisions you'll make. Although the prospect of an external opportunity can sometimes be more exciting, it shouldn't automatically be your first choice.

Every day you are showcasing your talents to your colleagues and managers and are investing your time and energy in the organisation and learning how it works and how it can work for you.

If you are working well, you have a great opportunity to develop trust with your manager and colleagues and to earn a reputation for reliability, integrity and high performance.

This knowledge of the organisation and the relationships you build can assist you in performing to a high level, which in turn further improves your reputation and confidence. In this way, you avoid having to 'start again' which happens when you move to a new organisation. It's generally accepted that it can take up to a year to settle in with a new employer and start to contribute which could stall your progress unless there are other career benefits to compensate.

Although it does depend on the size, style and performance of your organisation, you potentially have access to multiple opportunities there compared with (usually) one for each external job application.

These opportunities can come in different forms:

Promotion
This is the most sought after internal move – a new position with usually additional responsibility and/or an increased operational or functional responsibility. It is usually obtained as a reward for excelling in your previous position and because you are perceived to have the qualities needed to fulfill the new role.

A more senior position brings increased status and usually better financial rewards as well as providing new challenges and relationships and the chance to test yourself at a higher level.

Lateral move to a different position

Be open to a lateral move to a different position if it enables you to acquire new skills and experience that will be useful in achieving your career goals. Alternatively, it may introduce a new set of opportunities that interest you and cause you to change your career goals. Certainly you want to ensure that it is a logical move and doesn't compromise the investment you have made in your organisation.

Expand your responsibilities or take on a new project

Sometimes if it's not appropriate to change positions but you wish to develop your experience, this can be done by expanding or reconfiguring the responsibilities and boundaries of your current role. This is best achieved through a discussion with your manager so that the initiative doesn't backfire on you. You can develop your skills and at the same time demonstrate your ability to add value to the organisation.

It may need a change of attitude and approach on your part because unless you can lose some of your duties to a colleague, your day-to-day workload will increase.

Alternatively, volunteer for a project that interests you, that will improve your skills and is sufficiently high profile to enhance your credibility if completed successfully. Beware though that if the project goes wrong this could be detrimental to your reputation and progress within your organisation.

Developing skills outside work

Sometimes a steady job with manageable hours and responsibilities can be ideal for a year or two if you wish to add skills and knowledge outside of work that can enhance your career. This may include developing your conceptual knowledge through further education, learning a new language or technology, or simply becoming physically fitter.

Each one of these initiatives can impact positively on your performance at work and potentially advance your career.

Scaling back

Choosing a job with fewer responsibilities or at a lower level in the organisation is not an obvious career advancing move but it could be necessary in order to invest more time in other parts of your life. It may also enable you to recharge your batteries in a less stressful position prior to resuming your career.

However long you stay with your current organisation, your time there will be scrutinised by future employers. They will view promotions and logical lateral moves as evidence that you were/are a valued and able employee which will certainly make you a more attractive proposition for them.

Being as good as you can be

As discussed previously, your approach to your career management should be to make yourself as unique as you can so that the supply of your combination of skills and abilities is limited and in demand by the market. You need to remain up to date and employable.

This means taking a systematic approach to becoming as good as you can be in your day-to-day work and ensuring that your collection of knowledge, skills and abilities is honed to the highest level you can practically achieve.

Each internal or external appointment is made because the hiring manager is satisfied that you fulfill the following criteria:

→ You can do the job – your knowledge skills and experience are a close fit.

→ You want to do the job – you have the drive and motivation and it's a move that logically fits into your career plan.

→ You will fit well within the culture of the team and the company.

The emphasis may change for different positions and at different levels within the organisation. For example, when recruiting junior executives, organisations place much more emphasis on academic and technical skills rather than management and leadership qualities just because that reflects the nature of the work at that level.

To ensure you fulfill the above criteria, you should work on developing a 'Triple A' pedigree in the following areas:

Attributes (you can do the job)
Your attributes include your knowledge, skills and experience.

→ **Knowledge.**
Organisations look for evidence of your general and specific knowledge because they will recognise that you understand the theoretical concepts that apply to your position to a required standard. Depending on the position, they will want evidence of school certificates, university degrees and professional qualifications. Once you progress to mid-career positions, further studies and qualifications can be a useful indicator that you remain conceptually up to date. It's significantly advantageous to take qualifications/second degrees that you can apply to your day-to-day work and that are relevant to your career progression.

→ **Technical occupational and technology skills.**
Demonstrating technical or occupational competence (ie being good at what you do at work) is a very important foundation stone to a successful career because as your work is valued and trusted, your manager will feel comfortable in giving you more responsibility and greater scope to do your work. As a result, you will grow your boundaries of responsibility

and become more confident in your own ability to take on more complex projects.

Similarly, being able to use technology to your advantage will enhance your reputation. You need to develop the technical and technology skills as broadly and deeply as you can within your current job and then attempt to do the same in future positions.

As your career develops, the ability 'to do' assumes less importance but the ability to comprehend and solve technical issues remains essential, as does the ability to implement through others. It's harder to demonstrate your technical competence off the job in your résumé and in interviews but you must learn to be able to explain the concepts, the related issues and be able to discuss solutions.

→ **Language skills.**
Increasingly, employers seek candidates that are able to communicate fluently in different languages relevant to your location. Written as well as verbal skills are important, as you will often need to make presentations to others as well as converse with other offices overseas.

→ **Communication skills.**
These skills (sometimes termed soft skills) are an extension of you and your drive and values, which also impact on *Attitudes* and *Adaptability*. However, they can and should certainly be developed and improved and so are included here in Attributes. In particular, you need to focus on improving the following communication skills:

- → Verbal
- → Written
- → Listening
- → Social

Possessing these skills allows you to progress from technical roles to positions of responsibility with broader people and project management responsibilities. While it's more likely that you will be promoted internally to a more senior management position rather than externally, particularly in the current economy, possessing good social skills will set you apart from 80 per cent of your competitors. Such skills are on show during the interview process.

Attitudes (you want to do the job) and Adaptability (you fit in with the team)

Your attitudes and adaptability are determined by your personal characteristics (positive attitude, integrity, drive, ethics, values) and, again, you are the architect to changing and developing these characteristics.

Your ability to influence and lead others is critical to your long-term career success and it is the quality of your values and personal characteristics that will determine this.

Successful management and leadership are usually fashioned by qualities such as ethics, honesty, integrity, trust and ambition as well as having a positive attitude, creativity, impact and usually determination and persistence. Sometimes those in command use these qualities in negative as well as positive ways but nevertheless they are usually present and usually evident from the earliest stages of their career.

Certainly at the senior levels of an organisation people are hired or appointed on the basis of trust and their ability to make an impact on the business.

Whatever the position and level of seniority, a positive attitude is the key quality required in any new appointment because a positive attitude and a passion for one's work can override deficiencies in experience or knowledge. There is also a belief that in the current poor economy, passion is infectious and hugely beneficial to the morale and wellbeing of an organisation. Perhaps the most important aspect of this is that passion and attitude are not exclusive to those with an education or those working for the biggest and best companies. Indeed, they are qualities any of us can acquire and adopt.

Make your performance appraisals your scorecard

Most organisations have some kind of performance appraisal or management system to assist in an individual's assessment and you should view such a system as an excellent aide to you developing your career. You should use it as the platform by which to discuss and agree with your manager on the goals for the next period and then at the end of each period to jointly assess the quality of your performance.

In your initial review, try to have a two-way discussion about the long and short-term vision and goals of the company and division and how your role is important in achieving these goals. Discuss, if you can, how you will approach the role, what additional resources, if any, you might need and what performance levels will be required of you by your manager.

Such a conversation will provide you not only with a valuable framework within which to work but also will reaffirm the company's vision and goals and your manager's approach and style, all of which will impact on your desire to stay or move on.

Ideally every quarter and then formally each year, review your performance against the target and your progress against your career plan. Determine with your manager how the two of you can more effectively work together and then analyse your position and make the necessary adjustments to improve your skills and experience. This could just be you changing the way you work but it could also involve training and development or additional resources.

If your organisation doesn't have such a system or if it's not properly implemented then establish your own system. Ask for a quarterly meeting and then work through a checklist similar to the above with your manager.

Negotiating a pay rise

Different economies provide different conditions for pay advancement. Below are some techniques to ensure that you are able to negotiate a rise at the top range of your expectations.

Know the market conditions and market rates – know your value

Market conditions obviously have a significant effect on your salary and whether it's likely to rise or fall. When the supply of labour is high and demand poor there is a strong market pressure for salaries to fall. When the economy improves and skilled labour becomes scarce, the market forces push salaries higher. It's important to be aware and be sensitive to what is happening in the employment market and also to what you are worth in the market. You can usually find out this information from job advertisements on the internet or in newspapers or through recruitment consultancies.

Know the company position

Knowing the company's position on salaries and headcount and its financial health will provide you with more information on how to negotiate. Understanding the company's position will give you clues on how to approach the discussion. You should always aim to appear sensitive and understanding to the company's position, even if you are negotiating a rise.

Be clear on how you have performed over the past year – quantify benefits and have examples – and how you can add value over the next year

The single most important factor on securing a pay rise is you, how you have performed over the past year and how you feel you can add value over the next 12 months.

Obviously, the better your performance the stronger your chances of securing a rise. If you have been a mediocre performer, your employer will not feel under any pressure to reward you, particularly if you are paid at the market level. Identify specific examples over the past year where you have added value and performed well both for the company and your reviewing manager.

Similarly, it helps your case to be able to identify and outline specific ways in which you can add value over the coming year.

Identify additional responsibilities you can take on that would entitle you to a greater financial reward

If you can identify additional responsibilities that you can take on from other people and you can demonstrate that you can discharge those responsibilities effectively without affecting your overall performance, you will improve your case for a pay rise. Your employer will likely prefer to pay you more than go to the additional expense of employing someone else.

Ensure negotiations are friendly discussions rather than a confrontation

In your pay review, it's important that it is a professional and friendly discussion about your merits. You want your manager to be impressed not only by the merits of your case but the professional way you have presented yourself. While the conversation is friendly and amicable, you are likely to achieve this.

Negotiate on cash AND benefits

Sometimes it can be easier to negotiate an increase in benefits (parking or leave days, for example) than cash. If you think it will be difficult to achieve an acceptable cash increase then identify a benefit that is of value to you and could be awarded because of your position (be mindful that it would not set a precedent for the company). If you can't obtain a cash or benefits increase, try to discuss opportunities where your improved performance over the coming year can be rewarded by way of a bonus.

Negotiate in turmoil
When a company is in turmoil (departure of key executives, loss of major contracts, etc) it can be a good time to negotiate a permanent or temporary (by way of loyalty bonus) increase. Your manager may be pleased to have some certainty and be willing to pay for your loyalty.

Reasons to leave

In this chapter we have focused on internal opportunities but sometimes moving externally may indeed be the best career move for you. It's useful to construct your own checklist of reasons you would leave the company. Each person has a unique set of reasons but the following could be signs that it's time to move on:

Poor relationship with your manager
The way you work with your manager is crucial to your enjoyment, motivation and success. Like anything, managers range from poor to great and you have to hope that you work with one that is at least fair and competent. Try to be as adaptable and flexible as you can, discuss your situation if you can with your manager and, if not with them, then with another respected manager. Work on finding a solution.

If all else fails, then you may have to leave. The unfair aspect of a poor manager is that often potential employers will implicate you even though you may feel you are the victim. This is why it is important not to explicitly criticise your manager in a job interview. Instead, think of another plausible reason for leaving.

It's particularly difficult and unfair if it happens more than once in your career because potential employers probably begin to see a pattern that leads back to you.

Undervalued
Being recognised and valued for your contribution is vital for your career wellbeing and progression and if, over a prolonged period of time, you genuinely feel there is a lack of recognition by the key people in your organisation, it may be time to move to a more inclusive and appreciative environment.

Lack of responsibility or flexibility
Corporate style is an important contributor to you staying or moving and particularly the recognition that once you have earned the right through positive performances you should have more responsibility and flexibility in your role. This is usually evident in the degree of supervision and direction in your work from above and the lack of flexibility to enable you to work in the way you desire. Sometimes it's a temporary phase as different managers assess your competence and ability in different ways but if it's a long-term feature, it is another sign that it's time to go.

Lack of resources
Often the approach of a company to its internal environment can be indicative of its approach to its people including you. If it's poorly resourced with limited and outdated equipment in a poor working environment then it may not have the resources to invest in you or your future training and development.

You don't fit the culture
Corporate culture varies in style and strength between organisations and some suit more than others. Essentially, the more experienced and senior you become, the more culture impacts on your day-to-day working life.

If the company's and your own values and personal characteristics begin to clash on a regular basis, then your long-term future becomes threatened because you will be uncomfortable in communicating visions and values you don't believe in.

Remuneration
While remuneration should not be the only reason to move, it

certainly can be a contributory factor if some of the above conditions are not right.

> **TAKE ACTION**
> 1. Stay up to date and employable by becoming as good as you can be in your day-to-day work and honing your knowledge, skills and abilities.
>
> 2. Don't underestimate the power of a positive attitude and a passion for your work when it comes to how you are perceived by current and future employers.
>
> 3. Use your performance appraisals as tools to improve.
>
> 4. Prepare concrete examples of your worth before asking for a pay rise.
>
> 5. Recognise the signs of when it's time to move on.

Chapter six

Moving externally – application letters and résumés that work

What is a résumé or CV?

A résumé (often called a 'curriculum vitae' or 'CV' for short) is a written summary or profile of you and your career to date, listing your educational and professional qualifications, your employment record and any other information about you that may be relevant to a potential employer.

However, it's more than a record of your basic information – it's your 'advertisement' and marketing document selling you, your features and benefits to the outside world.

The objective of application letters and résumés

The objective of your résumé and application letter is purely to secure a meeting, or interview, with your prospective employer.

Your résumé and application letters are important in selling you to people who don't know you. It's their first impression of you and so needs to be a positive one if you are to progress further.

Ideally your résumé and application letter should be specific to each application and have sufficient impact in their appearance and content so as to persuade the reader of your résumé to want to meet you. In most recruitment assignments, an executive doesn't have the luxury of time. They will spend 10-15 seconds looking for reasons NOT to consider you further. If they can't find what they are looking for in your résumé, they will not consider interviewing you.

Application letters that work

Application letters are the packaging to your résumé – they are occasionally read but usually are only skimmed for relevant information or discarded altogether. They are relevant because they describe the reason or context of the résumé but they do need to be brief – a long general essay about your skills and experience, goals and aspirations will almost certainly not be read.

Ensure your letter is properly addressed, is referenced to a specific job that has been advertised or that you would like to undertake and that it confirms your interest and fit for the role. List three or four bullet points containing your attributes that you can link to the desired profile. State clearly your contact numbers and address.

If applying for a role internationally and it is not apparent from your résumé then state clearly that you possess a valid work visa to work in that country. If you don't have a valid work visa, this will be a deterrent to potential employers so it may be best not to highlight it on your résumé until they are interested in you for other reasons.

How to prepare a great résumé

Your résumé is a vital component in your job search. A powerfully written, visually appealing, impressive résumé is the one most likely to win you an interview.

The best way to achieve this is with a stylish two to three page résumé that highlights who you are and what you have accomplished. It should emphasise your most favourable attributes but also convey what value you can add to the job and the organisation.

In the same way you would present different answers to different exam questions, you should also tailor your résumé to each job application. You are not cheating, or shouldn't be, just matching the needs of your potential employers with your own attributes.

During your career you should retain a scrapbook containing all your résumés, details of important accomplishments, performance appraisals, job descriptions and important memos which you can scan and cut-and-paste to produce the résumé and profile you require. Your résumé will also change over time as you change and your career progresses from school and university to mid- and mature-career stage. This scrapbook will save you valuable time during your job search and career.

Although an effective résumé can be produced in any format, I recommend the reverse chronological format. In my experience, employers are very interested in your employment history and the development of your skills and experience over time and in different environments.

When reviewing your résumé, the reader usually begins by looking on the front page of your résumé for reference points that encourage them to look at the content of the other pages. These reference points correspond to their 'desired profile' which will hopefully be in their job advertisement or briefing to their executive recruiter. If you have sent a résumé to them speculatively and not in response to a specific advertisement, then you will have to guess their desired profile and reference points.

They want to be able to see these reference points quickly and easily. If they can't, they won't bother to read any further.

The front-page reference points are likely to include:

→ **Your name and contact details.**

→ **Education and training**. These are important to employers so you should list your degree(s), relevant courses, dates of graduation and the educational institutions for each. Mention any special honours, scholarships or awards received. Also add details of special or relevant training courses, especially those attended overseas.

→ **Professional qualifications.** Your professional qualifications, designations (with full name if uncommon) together with date of admittance or qualification.

→ **Technology skills.** Include advanced technology skills that could be relevant to the position in question or organisation together with level of proficiency.

→ **Language skills.** Include languages with degree of proficiency in reading, writing and speaking.

→ **Career summary/objective.** This should be a short paragraph of 15-20 words describing who you are and what you have achieved to date in your career. Or, if you are at the beginning of your career or changing your career, it's more likely to be a career objective. You should of course ensure the summary or objective is relevant for your application for this specific position or company.

→ **Dates of employment (from/to in months and years) with employer and job title.** Provide a brief description of previous employers, particularly for any smaller, less well-known organisations. Provide your current title and if it's not readily apparent, then also a very brief description of what you do. You should briefly outline the scope of your current job's responsibilities, as this will describe to the reader the level at which you work.

→ **Achievements.** This is where you should put most of your effort because your achievements indicate the value you added to each role and employer and potentially can add to a future employer. Examples could include: increased team productivity by 20 per cent, reduced overheads by $1m per annum, increased sales by 17 per cent year on year, improved workplace safety by 120 per cent.

→ **Reasons for leaving.** Employers are interested in your

reasons for leaving organisations because it's a useful indicator as to your judgment and logic. In most cases, 'career advancement' or 'increased responsibilities' or similar are the safest reasons although of course you need to be able to substantiate these. If you have weak reasons for moving jobs and employers (eg. headhunted, higher salary) then leave them off your résumé.

Other important notes

In preparing your résumé, place your most recent experience first and make sure the experience is broadly relevant. In other words, include in your résumé only information that is job-related (or which provides clear evidence of a pattern of success) and which addresses the needs of potential employers.

Use action words
Since every word, phrase and sentence used in your résumé is important in creating an impression, it's important to use words and phrases that display strength and convey action. Such words could include: achieved, evaluated, established, reduced, planned, performed, and so on.

Don't overdo it
Even though you are selling yourself, the language you use in your résumé should portray you modestly, not arrogantly.

Spelling and grammar
Poor spelling or grammar can ruin an otherwise stylish and competent résumé. Rewrite and review your résumé until you are happy and then ask someone close and/or one of your referees to review it.

Appearance and presentation
Ensure your résumé is visually pleasing by selecting a format and layout that has plenty of white space in the margins, uses bullet

points to highlight key points and features a reader-friendly typeface such as Arial or Franklin Gothic Book. Don't use more than two typefaces but do use bolds and underlines for emphasis.

Most résumés are delivered electronically and are printed off by the interviewer. Sending a hard copy could be unusual and therefore make an impact, but do ensure it's printed on high quality white or cream paper.

What to leave out

Like most things, résumés have evolved in style and structure over time and will continue to evolve as social trends and conventions change.

Certainly, you can justifiably leave out details such as age, marital status, references and any physical disability. Details such as current and required salary, educational history and reason for leaving are open to debate.

Since the objective of your résumé is to win an interview, you don't want to give potential employers reasons to screen you out on the basis of a lack of information. They will always think the worst if they can't find the information they want and that will almost always count against you.

My personal view is that employers will want to know your approximate age and will guess this from your years of experience so it makes no sense to aggravate them by not including it. I don't think marital status or physical disabilities are relevant on the résumé although they of course may become so during the selection process depending on the position.

Some employers will ask for your required salary in your application and are selecting on this basis which, although short sighted, is a hurdle you have to overcome. My advice is to state your current (or last) salary so as to present a guide of your market worth with the phrase 'salary requirements negotiable depending on the position' which indicates a degree of flexibility on your part. This will satisfy most employers through the initial screening phrase.

Overcoming bad news in your résumé

In our working life we soon learn to promote our strengths and conceal our weaknesses and this is particularly so in résumés. The objective of your résumé is to secure an interview and this is made more difficult if your résumé contains bad news. Bad news is defined as any issue or problem that the employer can use to screen you out of contention for an interview.

While you can't afford to lie (because if the lie works you will be found out in the selection process), you can overcome bad news by stressing the positives and downplaying the negatives. Some examples are as follows:

Breaks in employment record
Potential employers don't like a résumé with unexplained gaps between full-time employment so it's important to fill the gaps with narrative to ensure your employment history is chronologically complete. You want to avoid them screening you out purely on the basis of their incomplete knowledge of your past.

Similarly, while it's illogical and unjustifiable, anything more than three or four months out of work starts to suggest a hidden reason and employers will often not interview you even though you are in all other respects a suitable candidate. Therefore, if it is early July and you left your last job at the end of April, it's fine to have April as the last date on your résumé. If you get to August and beyond, you need to change your résumé to reflect that.

There are subtle ways to conceal a period of unemployment and these can include:

- → Consulting or contracting. If you were undertaking some private consulting assignments this can also embrace periods where you were job searching and not working. Employers will usually only be interested in checking precise dates and experience where certain projects that are central to your application were undertaken.

- → Travelling. People do resign to 'fulfill a lifetime's ambition' to go travelling for six months or a year. Although potential employers are unlikely to want to see your passport for proof, it's preferable that you will have seen some of the sights. While it covers the problem of being unemployed, it raises additional issues about lost skills and the logic of not working. This is much more difficult to cover mid- or mature-career than earlier in your career.

- → Further study. Some people do cover gaps through enrolling for further study. This is a legitimate technique for upgrading your skills as well as concealing difficulties in your job search from your résumé.

- → Sabbatical – only relevant in senior positions. Senior executives who have worked for say 15-20 years before a gap in their employment can and do claim that they have been taking a sabbatical (an extended vacation for a period of time). Some employers will be cynical, others understanding. There is no consistent perception. In trying to conceal gaps in your résumé you are essentially choosing the lesser of two evils as employers may still have question marks about your rationale in choosing to, for example, travel or study.

Too many moves in your career

Too many moves with different employers can prove a deterrent to future employers as they may perceive you to be opportunistic and greedy which are not sought after qualities in new employees. They will be wondering whether, after spending time and money investing in your induction into the business, you will leave for somewhere else.

Sometimes, of course, several quick moves can be the result of bad luck as employers go out of business or you are made redundant for commercial (as opposed to performance) reasons.

In order to reduce the poor first impression you can combine several jobs under a heading 'Early Career' or 'Mid Career' with the details of the companies and positions underneath. You should try to construct a logical pattern of reasons for leaving each job. Alternatively, you can suggest that the jobs were contract rather than permanent roles although this is not always recommended.

We would not suggest the use of 'functional' résumés, which focus on skills but not employment history. In our experience employers are cynical of functional résumés.

Too few moves
This is not as bad an issue to overcome although some employers may be concerned that you haven't been exposed to a variety of situations and circumstances if you have worked for the same company for, say, over 10 years.

You have to show that you have been promoted and transferred to work in different positions gaining a broad range of skills and experience. If you have been in much the same role you should demonstrate that you have been able to expand and grow the role.

Experience gained internationally
One of the challenges in marketing international experience is that potential employers may not understand its precise relevance to the local market. You will have to educate them and provide lots of information and reference points about your previous employers, such as a narrative to describe their business sector, line of business and turnover.

It's also vital that you include details of skills or experience that may be in demand locally but not widely available as this can help build a bridge between you and potential employers.

Career change

It's easier to change career in a boom economy rather than a depressed economy as skill shortages encourage employers to take bigger chances on staff, but generally employers want to hire candidates that are a close fit to their desired profile with a track record of success in a similar capacity. This is particularly so for mid- and mature-career positions. So it's likely that your résumé won't sell you into the position – you will need to try to meet with employers another way such as through a referral. However, on your résumé you will need to help yourself by being specific about the skills and experience you possess that are relevant for the role and also the skills and experience that may add to your application in a slightly different way from the norm.

For example, if you were a nurse who now wishes to be an accountant you will need to enroll in accounting degree courses and are more likely to secure a role in a medical services or pharmaceutical company. So, applications to such companies should reveal your previous history and should feature prominently in the résumé.

Making your résumé stand out

If you want to make your résumé stand out and look distinctive either in its appearance or by adding other documents, you may certainly interest and excite the reader enough for them to invite you in for an interview. However, you also run the risk of alienating your readers. There is no way of knowing which is the more likely response although big clues are the position, the business sector and the company's brand.

If it's a Financial Controller position with a conservative bank, it's going to be more of a risk than a marketing position with an advertising agency.

For most creative opportunities, you will be required to bring your work portfolio to the interview and for these and other positions you can add other documents to your résumé to create a portfolio for your application. These extra documents could include media articles about you or by you either in in-house brochures or external publications, extracts from your performance management appraisals or client testimonials. For positions in the engineering and architectural industries, you may wish to list your projects and related information about them to display not only your versatility but also your fit to the position in question. Such an addendum to your résumé could be 4-5 pages if you have enough material.

One final point on making your résumé look different from others. Many people download résumé pro formas from job sites. Although they are easy to use, your résumé will look the same as many others. This is not bad but if you want to look different you need to use a style that is a little more creative and individual.

Multi-media résumés

An increasingly popular trend is to prepare a multi-media résumé to send to potential employers via an internet link or DVD. A multi-media résumé is a short (ideally no more than 3-4 minutes) profile on you that encompasses both sound and vision, stills and video. The risks and potential returns of such an approach are much greater than with normal résumés. A well-presented visual promotion that presents you as an appealing, engaging person and highlights your professional record will be much more impactful than words on a page. However the potential to disenfranchise the viewer by portraying you and your character in the wrong light is also much greater in 3D and video.

This was highlighted for me recently in the reaction of a senior executive in a large multi-national company who dismissed such an application out of hand accusing the individual (unfairly I thought) of being a 'bigheaded fancy pants'. No matter that this was an unreasonable view – it was the view of the decision maker.

My advice is that multi-media profiles are worth considering as one tool in your branding armoury but should not be your only tool.

Update your résumé regularly

It's important to ensure that your résumé is up to date and reflects accurately the skills and experience you possess and the stage of your career. At least once a year, ideally as part of your Career Audit, you should review and if necessary rewrite your résumé even if you are not actively seeking a new position.

Ten don'ts on résumés

In my job as an executive recruiter, I see hundreds of résumés every month. These are some of the obvious don'ts:

1. **Don't forget to include your contact numbers and address.**
   The reader of the résumé needs to be able to contact you.

2. **Don't forget to identify your education and professional qualifications.**
   Employers are very focused on education and training so include comprehensive details of your course and institution.

3. **Don't include an incorrect career goal.**
   Including a career goal saying you are focusing on a career in marketing when you are actually applying for a logistics job makes you look sloppy.

4. **Don't make your résumé difficult to read.**
   The reader of your résumé won't bother to glance past the first page if it is poorly styled and structured – it needs to be

easy to read.

5. **Don't send an off-the-peg résumé to every application.**
   Make sure your résumé is specific to each application and includes the right skills and experience.

6. **Don't leave gaps in your résumé unexplained.**
   The reader of your résumé will assume the worst. Explain the gaps.

7. **Don't use 'headhunted' as a reason for leaving a prior job.**
   It's not a reason to move – just the mechanism by which you move.

8. **Don't make your résumé too short or too long.**
   Either can be bad. A one-page résumé doesn't get you through the door except for junior positions. Most employers will expect 2-3 pages. Similarly, very few résumé readers have the patience to read 5-6 pages unless you are a successful senior executive.

9. **Don't state the salary required on your résumé if you don't want to sell yourself on salary.**
   Simply state your current compensation (or last if unemployed) with the words (salary negotiable for the right position) in brackets.

10. **Don't forget to highlight your achievements.**
    It will be your achievements in your current or last job that will sell you into your next job so don't forget to sell yourself.

TAKE ACTION
1. Spend time crafting your résumé – it's your most powerful marketing tool.

2. Turn weaknesses into positives with clever (but not deceitful) disguises.

3. Stand out with an offbeat résumé … if you dare.

Chapter seven

The job search begins – where to look

Fifteen steps to a strong job search campaign

Even when the world economy improves the job market will become increasingly competitive and interviews harder to find. The objective of your job search campaign is to secure as many job interviews as you can to improve your chances of finding a job and a company that are attractive to you and good for your career. It means being organised and committed. Below are 15 steps to a strong campaign.

1. Establish your job search campaign
Applying for a few jobs you see on the internet and responding to occasional calls from headhunters is fine but it's not a job search campaign and it won't produce spectacular results. You should establish your job search campaign with both a physical and an emotional commitment.

Your physical commitment should be to establish your campaign headquarters. Ensure you have a desk, a computer with an internet connection and a phone (mobile or fixed) with voicemail so you can be contacted.

If you don't have a personal email address to send and receive emails, then set up one through an internet service provider. Ensure you select an email address that is relatively neutral – hotlegs@hotmail.com may be an apt description of you but it immediately presents the wrong brand image, particularly if you are applying for senior professional or executive positions.

Your emotional commitment is adopting a mindset that you are going to run a job search campaign that is organised, disciplined and persistent.

You need to be organised and disciplined in your job search so you know which companies and which jobs you have applied to and at which stage of the selection process you are at any one time. A recruiter or HR professional who calls you with an offer of an interview will sound far more reassured if your reaction is instant and positive rather than delayed while you struggle to remember which company or position they are discussing.

You should keep a file of each application with copies of advertisements, job descriptions, your research and notes of conversations.

Get into a routine so that every day you are reviewing each outstanding job file to ensure you have done everything needed to further your application, be it a call, an email, a letter or personal meeting. Ensure that you are generating enough daily activity to create more interest in you. If you are unemployed you should work at least 35-40 hours per week to find a job. If you are employed it is harder to cover as much ground but you can do most of your job hunting – research, cover letters and emails in the evenings and at weekends and arrange interviews for early morning or after work. You should aim for 10-15 hours a week, which is a similar workload to part-time study.

Set yourself goals and targets to buy newspapers, visit internet job sites, research company websites, phone your recruiters, market to target employers and talk with your network contacts.

Your targets should be achievable but the more active you are, the more interviews you are likely to secure and securing job interviews is the goal of your job search campaign.

Although statistics will vary depending on your skills and the position you are seeking, you will find that generally 200 marketing calls will produce 10 interviews, which will produce one job offer. Since ideally you want several job offers to give you a choice, you can see that you need to generate a lot of activity to achieve that goal.

Another tip is to keep statistics for each month of your job search of the number of advertisements applied for, the number of calls made to recruitment agents and your network, as well as the number of direct applications made and interviews attended for each category. This will help you in analysing the source of your interviews and, if necessary, be the catalyst to changes to your approach.

One of the most common reasons that job searches fail is a lack of persistence. If you don't make your target activity numbers day after day after day, then you won't secure many interviews which drastically reduces the likelihood of job offers.

You can't make excuses. You have to be committed and each day of committed activity brings you closer to that job offer.

2. Review yourself and what you are offering to the job market

Either as part of your career plan or as a reaction to a specific event, you have decided to seek another position and, since you are the most important factor in the process, it's important to review who you are and be very sure about what you are offering to the job market.

Review your self-analysis and the 15- to 25-word sentence that describes at least three of your special qualities that make you stand out from the crowd and which will be of interest to potential employers.

This is your career commercial, your advertising slogan, which you will use in your job search, in résumés, applications, telephone scripts and interviews to best describe you. Spend time on it to construct a slogan that you are happy to use.

Your special qualities may include:

- your professional qualification
- your degree
- your language skills
- your positive attitude and impactful personality
- your experience in a specific industry sector.

An example of a career commercial may be: 'An intelligent,

positive financial manager with fluency in Mandarin, Cantonese, Japanese and English and extensive experience in adding business value in the advertising and marketing sector'.

This analysis and creation of a career commercial not only helps you to better understand who you are and create a clear message that can help you secure interviews, but it also gives you confidence that you can be plausible and convincing in your job search.

This confidence will be a key ingredient in your success because hiring managers like confidence and look for confidence. Being confident will get you into situations you wouldn't normally experience and that same confidence will secure job interviews and offers.

Conversely, if you're not clear about your strengths or confident about your abilities, why should potential employers be?

3. Define your ideal job

Once you have reviewed yourself and defined the qualities you have to sell to the market, you need to define your ideal job. This may encompass some of your goal setting from your career management but will also involve some creative thinking and research.

In identifying your ideal job, your approach should be to build a bridge between your special qualities and what employers are seeking. If you can match their needs with your special qualities then you substantially increase your chances of securing an interview.

Using your special qualities as the reference points think about the job functions, industry sectors and types of companies that you think would be a good match for you. Using these in your research you will then identify specific executives within specific companies you can market to.

Preferably, your ideal job is one you are interested in and excited by because it will be playing to your strengths and experience but sometimes it doesn't because you wish to change career. It then becomes a little more difficult because you are trying to sell a proposition to the market that doesn't involve any or some of your special qualities.

4. Prepare your 'off the peg' résumé and application letters
It is important to prepare a general 'off the peg' résumé and application letter that can be provided on request but also be prepared to tailor your résumé to each application you make.

5. Calculate your financial constraints
If you are unemployed it's likely that you will have some financial constraints to your job search in that you will have a finite period of time to find a new job before your money runs out.

This has several implications for your job search – you have to be very focused at increasing your activity and you have to be more flexible in the range of jobs you consider.

If you are employed it is less of an issue but it is one you should still consider and calculate.

6. Don't resign from your job before your job search
Unless you have a very good reason for doing so, do not resign from your current job until you have another job to go to. Employers become unduly suspicious if you aren't working and obviously if you don't find a new job quickly it could cause some financial pressures.

7. The marketing plan – focus on the process
In order to find another job you need to identify and meet hiring managers who will be interested in your special qualities and who want to recruit someone like you.

You must use every method you can to locate those hiring managers and develop a relationship with them.

When people hire they do so because they think you can do the job and want to do the job but also because they like you and trust you and think you will fit in with them and their team.

Since this trust factor is so important in hiring decisions, being introduced by someone the hiring manager knows considerably improves your chances of being selected for interview. Even better if you know them personally yourself.

You may know the hiring manager from an existing relationship (you stay in regular contact) or a past-shared experience (university or previous employment) or they may have been introduced by a mutual acquaintance (referee, executive recruiter, friend or colleague).

If you don't know the hiring manager, then unless you are an obvious fit for the job you are less likely to secure an interview. Without any prior contact you somehow have to establish rapport and trust quickly either through the selection process (via an advertisement) or as a result of you contacting them directly. This can obviously be done – it's just a little more difficult to achieve.

There are five main ways to contact hiring managers who may or may not have active jobs:

→ Responding to job advertisements in the print media and job sites on the internet
→ Working through executive recruiters
→ Being introduced via your network
→ Making direct contact with potential employers
→ Other methods such as job fairs or campus interviews.

Research several years ago by US outplacement firm DBM identified that the percentage of successful searches for employment contacts were made through:

→ Responding to job advertisements   8%
→ Working through executive recruiters   11%

→ Networking 61%
→ Making direct contact with employers via their internet websites 6%
→ Other methods 11%
→ Not known 3%

The results from the survey show there are at least four clear approaches of finding a job. To maximise your chances you need to employ most or all of the approaches rather than relying on just one.

While each approach has different intricacies that we'll explore later on in this chapter, there are some common themes in your marketing plan, namely:

→ Using your 'matching' technique, prioritise your marketing so you focus on the most likely opportunities first.

→ Always focus on contacting the person you think will be responsible for making the hiring decisions. If in doubt, focus on the most senior people in that organisation and hope to be referred downwards to the hiring manager.

→ With your career commercial in mind, aim to present the hirers with a solution to their problem even if they don't know they have a problem!

→ Always be friendly and enthusiastic and confident in your marketing.

→ Asking for advice will be more successful than asking for a job. One approach is indirect and most people like to be helpful if they can. The other is too direct and challenges whomever you are speaking with. This is taking confidence too far.

Your marketing plan is your guidebook to securing interviews. If you can focus on the process outlined in your marketing plan and send enough résumés and applications with the right message to the right people, and if you can speak to enough of those right people, you will combine quality with quantity and secure interviews.

8. Research using the internet, your phone and the media

Good research will greatly assist your job search. The better your research, the more specific you can be with your marketing and the more knowledgeable you will sound to prospective employers.

The internet is an amazingly powerful research tool and through the search engines you can access information about industry sectors as well as the websites of individual companies.

You can add to your knowledge by calling people you know in relevant positions or people you have identified during your research and asking them for help.

This approach is more confronting than using the net but can be as rewarding because you can often glean additional or unusual information. A good telephone script will help you in this.

Increasingly, the newspapers and business magazines are highlighting business trends. A weekly review of the key media can assist in your research.

Whichever methods you employ, build a personal soft copy archive or an old fashioned but equally effective hard copy folder of relevant articles for future reference.

9. Perfect your telephone technique

The telephone is a powerful job marketing tool and you should use it as much as you can in your research, networking and marketing.

It is important because you can convey so much more of your personality in a telephone call than through an email and it's more likely that an executive will press the delete button than it is they will put the phone down on you.

Good telephone technique is essential for you to get the most out of your calls and you will be successful if you can build rapport with the person you are speaking with. People will be happy to help you if they can if they feel comfortable with the objective of your call and your manner and style. Usually you will have only 15-20 seconds to achieve this and, invariably, you will need a few calls and even a meeting for the person to open up to you.

Often executives are difficult to get to because they are guarded by their secretaries but some tips you can use to try to get through to them include:

→ Always find out the name of the person you want to speak to rather than just their functional title. You may be able to get this through researching company literature or their website or by calling reception and asking for the name of the person in the position you are trying to contact. Then call back later and, if you sound as though you know that person, you will most likely get through the receptionist and sometimes the secretary.

→ Try to befriend secretaries and enlist their help. Ask their advice on how and when you can speak with his or her boss. In my experience, being personable and sincere with personal assistants brings more success than being forceful and bombastic.

→ If the secretaries you contact are unhelpful, ring when they are not likely to be there (before and after working hours and at lunch times).

There is no right or wrong telephone script and you should adopt one you are comfortable in using which may take some time to practise and refine. Whatever your approach you should usually:

→ Introduce yourself by name
→ Mention that you are ringing for advice, and
→ Ask if it's convenient for them to talk.

This will take no more than 10 seconds and, if you can sound cheerful but businesslike, people will usually be open to talking with you. If it's not convenient for them, then ask if there is a better time and explain that you will call them back at that time (and then do so).

Asking for advice up front will instantly lower their barriers. The instant reaction of most people to someone they don't know will be suspicion and so their initial response will be a defensive one. Asking for advice disarms them and makes them more receptive to your next line.

This next line obviously depends very much on the purpose of your call, be it a research call about an industry sector or a call marketing your services as a prospective employee. Use open, probing questions such as:

→ What do you think are the growth prospects for this sector in the next few years?

→ Who is responsible for recruiting marketing managers within your company?

→ If you are selling yourself to a prospective employer then shape your script into crisp points using your 'career commercial'.

Always close your phone call by thanking them for their time and, where possible, ask for their email address so you can send them an email to say thank you. They then potentially become part of your network if you feel you can develop a relationship with them.

10. Be on permanent standby

When you have made several applications, whether through consulting firms, personal contacts or to companies directly, you are likely to receive emails and phone calls regarding these applications. First impressions are important so you obviously need to be very professional and courteous on the phone.

Sometimes this can be difficult if you are with other people or somewhere where it is difficult to listen and talk freely such as in the office or on public transport. However the caller will understand if you say that it is not convenient for you to talk but ask if you can call them back and then do so at the time requested.

Also be very conscious that managers and colleagues can guess that you are accepting a job brief on the phone by your mannerisms, questions and answers. If you don't feel confident that you will be able to conduct such a conversation without generating suspicion then arrange to call back. That is very acceptable and with mobile phones, very possible.

11. Maintain your confidentiality

Your view on the importance of confidentiality in your job search will determine the scope of your search.

If you are unemployed and keen to find a new job quickly, you will spread your net far and wide and be relatively unconcerned about who knows about your search, who receives your résumé and who talks to who about you.

However, if you are in a senior position with an organisation and you know your colleagues and superiors would look very unkindly on you looking elsewhere, then you will need to exercise the utmost discretion in your job search and guard your résumé and conversation about you with your life.

In practice, most people are somewhere in between the two but you have to take control because in most cities many people are connected in some way. That should work for you in your networking but against you regarding the confidentiality of your details.

12. Select your referees (and ideally mentors)
Throughout your career you should have people older and more experienced than yourself with whom you have a rapport and whose advice on your career you would accept and value. Ask them if they are willing to mentor you and, if appropriate, become your referee for job applications.

They don't need to be constant throughout your career and, indeed, as you develop it's important to have at least one referee who is or has been a manager or senior colleague and can provide potential employers with information and comments about you that have some credence and authority.

Most employers will make any offer to you subject to obtaining satisfactory references so if you haven't already done so, identify your potential referees before your job search commences and discuss your plans with them. They will be a useful sounding board and will help you formulate your message to the job market. They may also know the company or be able to add some special advice. You will want to alert them to the possibility of being contacted – let them know the company and position you are being interviewed for so that they can be prepared to answer on your behalf.

It is important that you and your referees are promoting the same message to potential employers – any differences will detract from the strength of your message and the application itself.

13. Set yourself a realistic timeframe
It's important psychologically to accept that your job search may take several months or longer because by setting a realistic timeframe you'll help yourself to stay positive and motivated for longer.

14. Ready, steady, go

Your preparation has been thorough but now it's time to start your job search. You need to spread your net and search for opportunities through these methods, which we will examine in more detail later this chapter:

- Respond to newspaper classified advertising.
- Surf the internet job sites.
- Use your network.
- Use employment agencies and executive recruiters.
- Target private sector employers.
- Approach government departments and agencies.
- Attend job fairs.

15. Staying positive

When you start your job search you do so with a great deal of confidence but if you experience several weeks without interviews or even acknowledgements to your applications, your enthusiasm can easily wane. If this becomes several months without any apparent success then it's easy to become despondent. This can become a downward spiral because your lack of confidence will be portrayed to potential employers and your persistence will start to falter.

Here the support of your family, friends and referees is important. By discussing your job search with them you will hopefully obtain useful feedback and maintain your confidence. Your monthly job search statistics are also helpful as you can analyse your contact rate and the success of your various job search methods.

So don't give up. Every day of your job search gets you one day closer to your next job offer.

Respond to newspaper classified advertising

Classified advertisements placed in newspapers are still a popular method of finding a job, although increasingly they are used for senior or specialist roles only.

When responding, tailor your application to the advertisement ensuring that your application letter and résumé address the desired profile. The more deviation from the position description, the less likely in the current environment that you will receive a positive response to your application.

Surf the internet job sites and place your résumé online

If you are an active job seeker you should use the internet to look for jobs either via job boards or on the websites of companies or executive recruiters you wish to target. The job boards are not only a good source of live jobs but they are also an effective research tool because you can learn from advertisements about the competencies required by companies in your current position or positions later in your career.

The internet is a powerful and popular method for finding jobs by not only applying to online advertisements but also by filling out the job alert profiles to ensure you receive regular notification by email of jobs that interest you. In addition, many job boards also have résumé databases where you can place your résumé for potential employers to access but be mindful of the potential breach of confidentiality when posting your résumé in a public place for all to see.

Companies are increasingly using filtering processes, however, and it can be difficult to project your specials skills through these. There are also software packages that are in use that allow résumé databases to be searched for specific skills and the frequency of the wording of those skills in your résumé can determine whether your résumé is selected or ignored.

One of the benefits of the job boards and email is that it's relatively quick and easy to make multiple applications but since this applies to everyone you can be sure that most jobs receive huge numbers of applications, which reduces your own chances of winning an interview.

Use your network

Increasingly, companies around the world are actively seeking referrals to friends or acquaintances of current employees and you may be able to access these companies via your network.

Your network is the group of people that know you and also the group of people who knows that group of people who know you. You are more likely than not to find your next job via your network. It is therefore important that you understand and learn the theories and techniques that will improve the quality of your networking.

Ideally, you should begin to develop your network at the start of your career and spend a lifetime investing, developing and extending it. Your investment will be repaid handsomely throughout your career via opportunities and recommendations.

However, if you haven't developed a network before this job search, you need to do so and the principles are much the same as beginning the network early in your career.

One word of caution regarding confidentiality for those job seekers who are currently employed. If your search has to be highly confidential because of the sensitivity involved, be very careful about the extent of your active networking. The more people you talk with, the more public your job search will be and the more likely it is that your employer will hear of your intentions. This is obviously less or not important if you are currently unemployed.

There are three core elements of networking:

→ You create the network.
→ You make a healthy connection with each contact.
→ You stay in contact on a consistent basis.

This is very similar to growing a successful plant or flower. You plant the seed or small plant, you ensure the surroundings (soil and sunlight) are conducive to growth and you then ensure the plant is watered regularly.

You create the network
You can quickly develop your own network by compiling a list of contacts that you think may be able to assist you or who may know people who can assist you in your job search.

These people can be family or friends, current or former work colleagues, former school or university friends and people you may have studied with through your apprenticeship or professional studies. Indeed, university alumni and professional association groups are fertile grounds for networks. Also work through your collection of business cards and consider business contacts such as clients, salespeople, bankers, lawyers and accountants as well as human resource managers.

The key here is to identify people you would feel comfortable in contacting initially and then ideally on a regular basis. Even if they seem unlikely contacts in the context of their job they may well know someone very relevant.

Many organisations now have employee referral schemes which encourage and reward (if hired) introductions to potential employees so many more people understand and are receptive to the concept of networking for jobs.

Aim to collect considerable information on each contact (names, telephone numbers, email addresses, their employer and perhaps their PA's name). Try to also collect relevant anecdotal information (family members' names, hobbies and interests) that will help you make a healthy connection.

Whether you use a spreadsheet, database or notebook is up to you but ensure that you are organised and systematically record key information in a manner you can easily access.

Make a healthy connection with each contact

One of the essential objectives when developing a new relationship or reacquainting yourself with an old contact in your network is to ensure the contact feels the dialogue and relationship is two-way or at least has the potential to be two-way. You want and need to project that you are likeable and that you can also be a worthwhile contact to them in the future – that you are not just a 'taker' looking for a job lead. If this is the case, then the contact will be much more inclined to help you.

Always begin your initial conversations with a reference point (we met at XYZ company or Mr ABC whom we both know referred me to you, etc) and then your situation (probably citing your career commercial ie. experienced product manager with extensive retail experience seeking a new challenge).

Your next step should almost always be to ask their advice. The advice can be with regard to who is responsible for recruiting in their company or it could be a question about how they found their job (if it's a job you admire) or anything else that you feel is relevant to your job search. Most importantly, try to develop a dialogue by identifying subjects and themes of common interest where you may also be able to contribute to them in some way.

At the end of the conversation, thank them for their time and advice.

The alternative to this is that you ask direct questions about whether they have any job leads or know of anyone with job leads but the problem with direct questions is that they make most people uncomfortable and you may find that, although you have a courteous but negative response first time, by the time you have made three or four calls to that contact, the response is a little more detached and firmly negative.

You stay in touch

Throughout your career you should stay in touch with your friends and network at least twice annually and ideally on a more regular basis. Calls, meetings and emails are all good ways to stay in touch. Often alumni meetings or professional development seminars enable you to network without being overly pushy. Over a number of years you will be able to develop acquaintances and friendships that will provide a strong foundation to your job search when required.

A highly effective way to stay in touch with your network is to maintain a 'watching brief' for information you think they might be interested in. It could be a link to an article that relates to a discussion you had, a brochure regarding software or even restaurant reviews – just something that is relevant and displays thought on your part.

It will be an investment in your future and when the time comes and you are seeking a new role, you will have a network of people who will know you and appreciate you and be very happy to recommend you.

If you are developing your network just from the beginning of your job search it will be harder to make connections quickly but regular contact (in this case probably monthly) can still produce results if you can project a likeable and confident image. It's also helpful to avoid making finding a job the key reason for the call. Of course mention that you are still looking but have a primary objective for the call such as: 'I'm still seeking that role I talked with you about but the reason I called was that I saw one of your competitors advertising for a marketing role and wondered what you thought of them'.

Use your brand – social and business networking sites

A recent but hugely effective method of quickly increasing the size of your network and communicating your availability and suitability for new positions and opportunities to that network is the use of social and business networking sites such as Facebook, LinkedIn and XING.

These sites enable you to post your profile which can then be accessed by others in search of, among other things, potential new employees. The key here is to ensure that you maintain the consistency of your brand across all sites and that your postings on these sites are accurate and up to date.

Approach employment agencies and executive recruiters

Using employment agencies and executive recruiters (or headhunters) to help you find a job is common practice in North America, the UK and Australia but a relatively new concept in continental Europe, Africa and Asia.

Employment agencies and executive recruiters can open doors for you. They exist and flourish because they save organisations time and money in the recruitment process and protect the identity of the employer through the selection process. Their services are free to you the job seeker although there are guidelines to ensuring they are effective and these are listed below. Some firms will approach you if they have a job they think may interest you while others will want you to contact them when you are starting your search.

Know their objective

Many of the better recruiters are user friendly and will also be helpful in describing market conditions and assisting with your career plans.

However, remember that their client company is paying them and you should regard them as the outsourced recruitment division for your potential employers. As 'matchmakers' they will work to the 'desired profile' that their client has given them, which may or may not coincide with your profile. Also, while they will sell the benefits of a particular job or company to you they are less likely to draw your attention to all the potential pitfalls of the role or the company. This is not immoral or negligent but just a function of their role in the job matching process.

You just need to tailor your approach accordingly and assume responsibility for conducting your own research and due diligence in the same way you would do if purchasing a car, house or holiday.

Choose your recruiter carefully

Employment agencies and executive recruiters come in all shapes and sizes and, unfortunately, quality. Choose to work with a company (or companies) that you or colleagues or friends have had a good experience with. Alternatively, select a specialist in your discipline and one used to working at your level. For example, an executive search firm is highly unlikely to be able to help a graduate and a specialist accounting recruiter will have a more in depth knowledge of the accounting market than a generalist recruiter.

Bigger companies tend to be less personal than smaller firms but often will have more market coverage by virtue of their size.

Beware of the practice of some less ethical companies in sending out your résumé to companies without your knowledge. At worst it can breach your confidentiality and threaten your current employment, at best it can make you look unprofessional as your résumé is received by the employer from several different recruiters. Always insist that recruiters have your permission to send out your résumé to a prospective employer and that they are specific about the job or that it is a speculative approach to their client.

Make yourself easy to help
Whatever their level, size or market sector reach, executive recruiters are in business to place people in interim or permanent jobs and the easier you are to help or place, the more likely they will spend time assisting you with your job search. Again, this is simple business dynamics and no slight on you as a person or your experience or integrity.

Since they are going to assess you on your potential fit to their clients, help them (and yourself) by understanding your own strengths and weaknesses, your career goals and job search preferences. Ensure you communicate these clearly in the résumé and instructions you provide them.

If your application lacks clarity and professionalism and you appear to have unrealistic expectations, they will be less available to help you. Be user friendly to the recruiter and they will be user friendly to you and more effective on your behalf.

Use a referral to get you on the inside
All executive recruitment companies have a résumé processing system or procedure, which will filter you on or off their radar screen. Since they have limited time they will tend to want to speak to or interview only those people they believe they can help find a job in the foreseeable future.

However, since you are (hopefully) more memorable in person than on paper your objective should be to get an interview or meeting with one of the consultants and preferably one that can assist you directly in your job search.

In a face to face interview you will be able to communicate your strengths and preferences and project your personality. You have a much better chance of developing a rapport with the consultant and become a person not just a name.

A telephone conversation, while not as valuable as an interview, is better than no personal contact at all.

However, particularly in the current economy where jobs are scarce it can sometimes be difficult to get an interview so often a referral from someone known to that firm – a colleague friend or even referee – can help you secure a meeting.

If you don't have such a referral then contact the person from that firm who is handling the opportunities that appeal to you most. If you are enthusiastic and professional enough you are likely to persuade the consultant to meet with you. Alternatively call the chief executive of the firm and try to get a referral from them to the relevant consultant.

Stay in regular contact with the recruiter
Although some recruiters maintain regular or occasional contact with you depending on the status of your job search, don't rely on this. It's important that you take responsibility by having a 'contact program' whereby you telephone your contact at that firm at least every three months. This could be every month if you are active in your job search or possibly every week if you are seeking temporary or interim contracts. In this call just enquire about the job market, the progress of your application and let them know of any changes to your situation. If you have added new skills or experience then send them an updated résumé.

In this way you stay top of mind when assignments arise and increase your chances of being called about a specific opportunity. However, beware of overdoing it and becoming a nuisance as this can have an adverse effect.

Understand that you won't get selected for interview for some jobs you feel you are suitable for, but follow up just in case.

One of the greatest frustrations job seekers have with executive recruiters is that when they apply for jobs that they feel suited to on the basis of the information provided in the advertisement, they don't get selected for interview.

This can be frustrating but behind the scenes the consultant is usually working to a detailed brief from the client which will most likely encompass a wish list of skills and experience, a preferred career path to date as well as personal style required. Although it's unusual for the recruiter to put the whole contents of that brief in an advertisement, they will select for interview on those criteria.

Nevertheless if you feel mystified that you haven't received an interview, ring and speak with the consultant about your application. It may be that you have simply been overlooked or have not properly communicated your skills and abilities.

Target private sector employers

In the same way that you may be open to hearing about excellent career opportunities even if you are happily employed, managers of private sector organisations are invariably receptive to hearing about good people even if they don't have a specific vacancy. It's not usually near the top of their list of work priorities, however, which can make them appear disinterested.

Your objective is to find those line managers and get them so interested in you and what you can potentially offer them in the way of skills and experience that they want to meet with you and then ultimately offer you a job.

People meet and hire people they trust and like which is why using referrals from your network into line managers is such a powerful job search tool and why without such referrals your research and marketing skills need to be very good.

Your approach should be to research organisations that you want to work for and you think may be interested in you and your unique package of skills. What you are looking for is a bridge that somehow connects you with that organisation. It may be their country of origin and your language skills, it may be your unique combination of university degree subjects and professional qualifications or recent functional job experience. Whatever your unique package of skills, be creative in thinking about organisations that may be interested, then find out the name of the line manager you think would be responsible for hiring someone like you and use your telephone skills to ring them.

After confirming that they are free to talk, you must first confirm if they are responsible for hiring within their division and then do your best to sell yourself to them.

You should experiment with scripts and use one that works for you but an example may be: 'I appreciate that you may not be recruiting at the moment but I am seeking a new challenge and your organisation is one I would really like to work for. My expertise is (use your career commercial here) and I wonder if there would be an opportunity for me to meet with you briefly just in case something were to come up in the near future'.

What you are trying to do here is take any pressure off the line managers about committing themselves to hiring you but at the same time encourage them to meet with you.

If they do agree to meet you, then it's up to you to be so impressive in person that they will want to create a position in their team for you. Usually they will decline a meeting or refer you to their human resources manager.

If they decline then continue to remain upbeat and positive and ask them if you can send your résumé to them anyway 'just in case'. While this is bordering on being pushy, what you are hoping for is that once received your résumé will be read and stored for future use. You can use email or physical mail to send your résumés or both methods for added effect.

If you are referred to the human resources manager, then follow up ('Mr/Ms Line Manager recommended I speak with you …') with a call.

The reason that I don't recommend a first call to a human resources manager (unless, of course, it is an HR position you're seeking) is that they are generalist practitioners and so are unlikely to pick up on your specialist background and the special reasons that you would be of interest to the line manager.

Some people prefer to send their application letters and résumés and then follow up with a telephone call several days later and of course this can be just as effective.

Approach government departments and agencies

In most countries local, regional and national governments and their business enterprises are some of the biggest and most diverse employers. They offer many opportunities in a great variety of occupations and professions and generally have a comprehensive and objective structured selection process. Governments in most countries offer lots of information and easy access on their websites.

Attend job fairs

Job fairs are more common in some countries than others and are usually targeted more at entry-level opportunities and recent graduates than for respondents with considerable work experience or for senior positions. These job fairs are publicised in the newspapers and on internet job boards.

Consider the contracting and interim option

In Western economies it is common for employers to hire staff on a temporary, contract or interim basis to complete specialist projects, assist at a busy time or replace permanent employees who are on leave of absence. While this practice is more uncommon elsewhere, it is worth considering as a great way to network, learn new skills, and earn an income while you continue to search for a permanent job.

Organisations will usually pay you on an agreed hourly or daily rate for a fixed period of time although one of the common features of contract work is that it usually extends beyond the initial contract and sometimes becomes a permanent job. It's a great way to get into an otherwise difficult job market.

Work for free

If you are facing challenges in finding work, be open to working without pay for an organisation for a short period of time to showcase your skills and your positive attitude. Some employers will be prepared to give you a go but, unfortunately, others will take advantage of your enterprise and good nature. Nevertheless, if you can't find opportunities any other way it may be the only way to develop work skills and give yourself a chance at securing a permanent job.

Also consider undertaking volunteer work if you have been without work for some time. This can either be within your specialist occupation or the position you are seeking. It will assist you to acquire new skills and gain experience that can be used to gain more financially rewarding work.

Working internationally and the importance of visas

Working internationally is an attractive career option with some definite advantages and potential risks. It is not for everyone, however, and you should research this option much more thoroughly than you would a local move as you are investigating a lifestyle choice as well as a career move for you and any dependants.

Some of the questions you need to answer through your self-analysis and research are as follows: Why you want to go overseas (career advancement, adventure, financial reward) and what expectations you have for such a trip. Where do you want to go? Have you been there before either as a worker or a visitor? The critical factors will revolve around work visas, security, accommodation, language, quality and reliability of employer and work assignments and remuneration but there will also be other factors.

If you are going with your family and/or a partner, the considerations are that much greater. Then consider the reaction when you return to your local economy with one, two or three years' experience overseas. Will it be experience you can market easily or with some difficulty? Does that matter to you?

Luckily nowadays with the internet and technology in general, it is becoming much easier to research such moves.

Planned properly and undertaken positively and with an open mind, a stint abroad can be hugely beneficial to you as a person and to your career as it brings you a wide range of new experiences and skills.

From the employer's perspective, organisations are open to international recruitment especially where you have skills and experience not readily available in the local market. However, they also recognise the risks and costs of recruiting internationally and so will be assessing your potential value against whether you have a work visa and, if not, how costly and difficult it will be to get one, the risks attached to you or your family not settling in to your new environment, and your work styles being compatible and complementary to the organisation's local culture.

What if your campaign isn't working?

If your job search campaign isn't working and you aren't winning interviews after one or two months of your job search, it's probably due to one of a few reasons:

→ You have the wrong message. Re-analyse who you are and what you have to offer potential employers.

→ You have the wrong targets. Improve your research of the market and your potential targets. Ensure that you are building a bridge between your skills and what your target employers need or are likely to need.

→ You have the wrong approach. Review your telephone script, soften your personal style and improve your résumé.

→ You are just unlucky. Remain persistent, positive and confident.

> **TAKE ACTION**
> 1. If you are unemployed, dedicate 35-40 hours per week to finding a job. If you are employed, aim for 10-15 hours a week.
>
> 2. Build and maintain a network of useful contacts but be sure to make it a two-way street where you can potentially help each other.
>
> 3. Explore all avenues in your job search campaign – don't just rely on advertised positions
>
> 4. Perfect your telephone technique.

Chapter eight

Facing the interview – prepare and perform

Understand how the interview works

Interviews are still the most popular form of selection for most positions and since everything you do in your job search (planning, networking, résumés and so on) is done to win you an interview, it's essential that you perform in interviews to take advantage of your hard work in your job search and to generate job offers.

It's those individuals who perform well at interviews who are made job offers ahead of those who are perhaps better qualified but perform less well.

Good interview technique is vital to securing the top jobs and, like good exam technique, it can be learned and practised. You broadly will know before the interview how it will proceed and the questions that are likely to be asked.

The interview is also very important for your own assessment of the organisation, the job and the people and how their 'proposition' fits into your career plan. In the same way they will be assessing you, you must also assess them. Just because you perform well at the interview and they offer you the job doesn't mean that it's right for you or that you should accept it.

Although interviews come in all shapes and sizes depending on the interviewer, the organisation and the position itself, there are always three questions the interviewer will want to answer after having met you:

→ Can you do the job? (Do you have the necessary knowledge, skills and experience to be able to do the job to the standards required?)

→ Do you want to do the job? (Are you motivated to do the job? Does it logically fit into your career plan? Is there enough scope for you to develop the role?)

→ Will you fit into the team? (Is there a compatibility between you and the existing people in the team? Do you share similar values and visions?)

They will ask many different questions and form impressions from meeting you but, essentially, they will want to confirm in their own mind that you do, or don't, comply with those three basic questions. Similarly, you also want to answer those questions for yourself to determine whether it's a job you want to do and an organisation you want to work with.

Interviews are usually one on one (see below for comments on panel and group interviews) and, although the approach may differ, the structure is usually the same:

→ There is an opening period of a few minutes where the scene is being set and first impressions are being formed.

→ There is a middle period in which the conversation will embrace the organisation, the job itself and you and your potential fit. This is where you will be asked many questions.

→ The closing period, again a few minutes, will be an opportunity for the interviewer to summarise and to indicate the process from here. You will also be able to ask questions here if you haven't had a prior opportunity to do so.

In recent years, interviews have become more sophisticated as organisations have been striving to increase the link between interview success and workplace performance. Situational interviewing is now commonplace and it uses the premise that previous performance is a reliable indicator of future performance.

Questions related to your competency to perform the job to the required standard will be asked and will most likely revolve around how you have recently tackled situations you are likely to face in this particular role. You will be asked to describe the scenario, your actions and the outcome.

From your answers, your interviewer will be able to develop a picture of you and your potential fit to the specific role. They should ask all the interviewees a similar suite of questions to ensure consistency in their final analysis.

The style of the interviewer will greatly affect the style of the interview. Some interviewers will be more experienced in asking you the questions that enable you to promote your skills and abilities. There will be others where you have to guide the interviewer to ask you the questions you want to answer. There will be formal and informal interviews, interviews with structure and others without, some short and some long, although most will take between three-quarters of an hour and an hour and a quarter.

If you are interviewing with a line manager, they are more likely to focus on your ability to do the job (Can you do the job?), a human resources manager may probe the softer side of you (Do you want to do the job?), while a CEO probably will be more interested in your ability to fit the culture (Will you fit into the team?). Of course, each interviewer could explore all three questions in the one interview.

The more senior and specialist the position, the more likely you are to have more than one interview and with individuals who are from across functions and sometimes locations. Your objective should always be to project a consistent and positive message. Although you may be bored with your message by the time you have met the fifth person in an organisation, it will be the first time they have heard it. When those people interviewing you confer, one of the key drivers in their decision will be the consistency of your message throughout the process.

In some situations, you can be interviewed by a panel or as part of a group. Panel interviews can be difficult because the theme and style of the interview is often disjointed as two/three/four different people have different agendas and styles. The questions also tend to be more rapid fire as each interviewer lines up to ask a question. Your approach should just be to answer each question on its merits and not be too concerned about projecting your personality or developing rapport with the interviewer. This can come up at a later stage.

In group interviews you are being assessed on your role as a team member. Do you lead or do you follow? How and what do you contribute? Here you can do no more than present your natural style but ideally with an extra dose of confidence. Certainly don't try to dominate the session but listen and contribute selectively in areas where you feel you can add value and insightful comment and reasoning. If there are periods of silence, by all means lead the conversation but again only if you feel you have something valuable to contribute. You are being selected as much for the things you don't say as the things you do say.

Prepare yourself

There are two key secrets to interview success – preparation and performance. Before the interview you can do so much to enhance your chances of success. Take several hours prior to the interview to prepare yourself (ideally the night before because then you can sleep well knowing you are well prepared).

There are five areas you should review:

Review yourself and your 'proposition'
Between half and two-thirds of the interview will be about you, particularly your knowledge, skills, experiences and career goals. It's therefore essential that you know everything there is to know about yourself and be able to answer any question confidently and concisely.

You are likely to be probed about your past so you need to be able to describe and portray yourself in a positive and balanced manner. Review your career to date and understand your key skills and strengths, accomplishments and shortcomings, your reasons for making a move both now and previously as well as your short and medium-term career goals.

Ensure that you feel comfortable with your 'career commercial' and that you can expand on this to sell yourself confidently. This should be no more than a short refresher course prior to the interview as you should have already spent quite some time on a thorough self-analysis.

Research the job

It's important to spend time analysing the job advertisement or detailed job specification for two reasons. Firstly, is it a role that interests you (and if so, why) and can it help to advance your career? This has probably been answered, at least partially, affirmatively otherwise you wouldn't be attending the interview.

Secondly, how and where do your skills and experience match to the role and can you add value to the company in this position? The interviewer will be/should be focusing heavily on this latter aspect so it helps for you to be able to answer this question effectively.

Also write down any additional information about the job that you need in order to be able to decide on whether or not it's a position of interest. This will form the basis of any additional questions you have about the job itself.

Research the organisation – its products or services, its culture and vision

It may be that you have generated an interview with this organisation from your market research so you will already know much about them and why they are relevant to you.

However, if not then it's important to research them for several reasons. You want to know for yourself whether it's an organisation you want to work for in a sector you want to work in and you may also be asked a question or wish to ask a question about them.

A popular interview question is 'How much do you know about our organisation?' It helps your case enormously if you can respond with a brief summary about the company with some observations about its standing in your particular function. Although these observations will need to be more complex for senior positions, they are relevant at any level because they portray you as someone who is interested in and aware of the issues of the day.

To conduct your research, visit the organisation's website and access information about what they do, their products or services, markets, number of employees, sales volume, growth, competitors, their unique propositions, market reputation and financial standing.

Use the internet to search for recent articles that are about the organisation's performance, philosophy, culture or people.

Also ask friends and your referees what they know about the organisation and, if you have someone within your network that works there or has done previously, then ask their opinions of the organisation and the division you are interviewing within.

Research likely questions and answers

There will be questions back and forth on both sides and it helps if you have an idea about the questions to be asked of you by the interviewer. It's a similar process to knowing what the questions are before you take an exam. The questions asked are likely to be related to you and your profile, its relevance to this role and how you can add value both short and medium term.

Similarly, it is important for you to ask questions during the interview and you should research and prepare these beforehand. Your questions should be about the job, the company and the sector. A good one is to ask the line manager about their background and why they would be a good person to work for. Often, if you can get the interviewer to talk about themselves you not only learn more about them but they feel better about the interview and about your performance.

For more examples, read the section later in this chapter about asking and answering difficult questions.

Prepare yourself for the interview

There are a few finishing touches required to complete your interview preparation:

→ Ensure you will be dressed and groomed appropriately for the interview and that you will look as good as you can. Physical appearance and presentation is a very important ingredient in your likely success because your interviewer is likely to be influenced by your appearance as well as your intellect. It will also do your confidence no harm at all to look and feel good.

→ For the purposes of the interview, ignore the dress code of that organisation and dress in a professional and businesslike manner, wearing what you would expect to wear to meet an important client. Clean shoes and clothes that are relatively new are important and you must consciously make a decision on jewellery and make up. It's your choice but you have to assess and be comfortable with the likely consequences of you dressing a certain way.

→ While your interviewer should have copies of your résumé, take several copies with you just in case and ensure that you complete any application forms or other information required. Take a notebook if you wish to take notes during the interview.

→ Ensure that you know who you are meeting where and at what time. Know the directions and the time it will take you to get there. You don't want to arrive late and, although the interviewer may say it's fine, it can only detract from your own interview performance. Take the phone number of the person interviewing you so that if you are running late you can call ahead and apologise. If you are going to be very late you may need to rearrange the interview for another day to give you the best chance. Whatever happens, don't be late or cancel for a second time or you will test your interviewer's patience.

- As much as you can, arrange the interview at a time of day that suits you and your body clock. Give yourself every possible advantage to be able to perform at your best.

- Finally, with all your planning complete, prepare yourself mentally so that you feel energised and motivated by the interview and can perform to and beyond your capabilities. This interview has for you a similar significance to an athlete competing in the Olympics. Talk yourself into the right frame of mind which is feeling well-prepared, confident and excited, but a little nervous.

Perform in the interview

It has to be a performance. Not a theatrical performance but a confident, assured display that demonstrates your credentials for the job in question. You have prepared well and know broadly what you have to say. In the interview you need to build rapport quickly with your interviewer and you can do so by:

- Projecting energy, interest and sincerity

- Quickly analysing the interviewer's style and adjusting your approach accordingly. If your interviewer is very enthusiastic you should be so too. If they are more formal, then you need to tone down your energy without losing your enthusiasm

- Paying attention to your body language, particularly maintaining eye contact, which generates trust, confidence and credibility. Also, let your facial expressions reflect the flow and tone of the discussion, smiling where appropriate. Avoid pulling dramatic faces or making elaborate gestures

- Sitting with good posture in a relaxed and confident manner.

→ Listening carefully to comments and questions and answering questions thoroughly and, where possible, concisely.

It's preferable for the interview to be a pleasant and informative dialogue rather than a monologue or a quick-fire question-and-answer session. Some interviewers are good at achieving this, others aren't so good, which means it's partly your responsibility to ensure that it works this way. If the interviewer enjoys the meeting, they are more likely to think positively about you.

You should also expect the unexpected. You will have a plan but interviews rarely go as planned. Something usually goes wrong with the timing or location, the numbers of people interviewing, or the questions asked. Take such events in your stride. If you remain 'calm in a crisis' this will be to your advantage. Your prospective employer will view you as someone who can cope with unusual issues.

Finally, turn your mobile phone off prior to the interview because you risk alienating the interviewer and disrupting the flow of conversation if it rings. However, if you do forget and the phone does ring just calmly apologise and turn it off immediately without glancing at the caller ID.

The first five minutes

In the first five minutes your interviewer will form an impression about you that is rarely overturned so it's essential that you make a positive impact in the way you dress and the way you communicate. A smile, a positive greeting, good eye contact and a firm handshake really do matter.

Be prepared to conduct some small talk before the body of the interview in order to build a rapport with the interviewer before the important exchanges begin.

Answering difficult questions

Once the initial small talk is over, a dialogue should ensue about you and your 'fit' for the position in question. This is likely to revolve around the interviewer asking you questions about your knowledge, skills and experience. You can anticipate many of those and, as discussed before, they will fall in three broad categories – Can you do the job?, Do you want to do the job? and Will you fit into the team?

Whichever questions are asked of you in the interview, try to provide responses that portray you as capable and positive and someone who can add value to the role in question and to the company in the short and medium term.

Below are some of the trickier questions commonly asked and some guidance on how to answer them.

Tell me about yourself

This is usually used as an opening question and gives the interviewer an early indication of your style and approach. It's a relatively easy question to answer if you have prepared but you do need to proceed with extreme caution.

You should write a response to this question in preparing for your interview and rehearse your delivery so that it sounds natural. You will have done much of the groundwork anyway in your self-review and in preparing your 'career commercial'.

Be concise but informative in your response. Depending on your career stage, it should take 2-3 minutes and include the highlights and sometimes lowlights if they are plainly evident. Focus predominately on your professional career although include significant personal events and experiences if they have impacted on your career.

Ensure that you display your competence and interest in the position but don't give your life history – if the interviewer wants more detail about a specific incident or phase of your life they will ask for it in a later question.

What are your three key strengths and can you give me a recent practical example that illustrates each strength?
In almost every interview, a question about your key strengths or skills will arise although often it will be disguised. From your research you will know your strengths and in this and any questions about your abilities you need to relate it to the position you are interviewing for and be able to identify specific recent examples where you used this strength in your work.

What value have you added to your company in your current role and what value have they added to you? This is a good question to answer because it enables you to demonstrate your expertise in two ways. It's a double question, so you have to remember to answer both parts. Beginning with the first part, with employers seeking 'added value', this is essentially seeking your accomplishments in your current role.

It's important to be able to identify and quantify specific ways you have benefited your organisation and often the best way to approach it will be to outline the challenges or issues you faced in the role or the desired outcomes for the role when you started. Ideally you want to be able to find similarities between the challenges faced in your current role and in this role so that you can start convincing the interviewer that you are the solution to their problem.

In the second part of the question, identify how you have progressed and what skills and experience you have added to your profile. Employers like to meet people who are aware of key issues and who are perceptive of changing situations and this can be an indicator. Also, you have the opportunity to build a picture of yourself having improved to a situation where you are now ready – and very able – to take on this role.

What are your key weaknesses?

You can guarantee you will get a question on your weaknesses or negative experiences and it's difficult to answer. However you can turn this around to be a positive response.

In answering this question, more than most your body language needs to be first rate. Concentrate on speaking directly and confidently, maintain eye contact with the interviewer and avoid fidgeting or shifting in your seat, which could suggest you have something to hide.

The question will either be general, as above, or will relate to a specific incident or obvious negative in your history (such as a short stay or apparently bizarre move).

With regard to the general question, you should discuss a weakness that is sufficiently significant to answer the question satisfactorily but is not attitudinal and will not impact on your ability to perform in this role. In answering the question you also always want to describe how you are working to remove or negate the weakness, which also demonstrates a positive aspect because you are focused on self improvement.

With regard to a question about a negative event, be reflective and neither defensive nor apologetic. Every successful executive has had a negative experience they have had to deal with but they will have hopefully learnt and benefited from it. You are best to acknowledge the issue, outline what you learned from the experience, and emphasise how you moved on and the fact that you are a different person now.

For example, you may have stayed within an organisation for only a few months and be quizzed on this. It may have been due to a difference in expectations of the role between you and your manager which had arisen because this was not discussed in detail during the selection process. In this case you should explain that this was partly due to you not asking sufficiently detailed questions and you have since learned to be more thorough in most situations. You can obviously then demonstrate your newly acquired skill by asking good questions in this interview!

Tell me about a time when you displayed Characteristic X. What was the result? What was the outcome?

This often relates to the skills and abilities required for the role as indicated in the job specification or advertisement and so, before each interview, try to construct an answer related to their specific requirements. They are looking for recent real life examples of you displaying initiative, leadership or perhaps specific technical skills.

Is there anything you would have done differently in your current role?

This is a chance to outline mistakes you may have made or discuss lost opportunities and often it's prudent to do so as you can then portray your human side. You can also demonstrate that you are analytical and that you learn from your mistakes. However, ensure that your observations don't portray you as negligent or careless. It's a delicate question and requires a well-considered response.

Why did you make the move from Organisation X to Organisation Y?

Employers are looking for new hires that make well-considered and logical decisions and career decisions can be indicative of one's broader behaviour. They will look for a pattern and will like the fact that you made a considered move to gain broader skills or to accept greater responsibility.

Taking a risk that didn't pay off or having a short stay is not an issue so long as your reasons for making the move were sound at the time. However, being headhunted is not a reason for moving and be careful not to emphasise disputes with managers. Also employers are increasingly rejecting candidates whose motives have been purely financial or who have a series of quick moves on their résumé.

What are your reasons for wanting to move on from your current position and organisation?

Like the last question, it's important that you provide a logical reason for wanting to move and you do need to be able to demonstrate that you want to move your career forward and ideally that this position and company can help you with this.

Acceptable reasons for leaving might include a lack of opportunity or challenge, poor compensation, corporate changes and unacceptable working conditions. Avoid making any negative statements about your colleagues and certainly your line manager unless a poor relationship with your line manager is fundamentally your reason for leaving. If it is then you need to be specific about the issues and be able to describe them objectively. If you have a series of bad experiences with managers be aware that potential employers will perceive this negatively.

If you are currently unemployed you need to prepare thoroughly for this question. Employers may think the worst (that you have been dismissed due to poor performance) until you can allay their fears.

Ideally your redundancy was due to reorganisation or restructure or the position changed substantially, making your skills and abilities less relevant for the role. You will need the help of your previous employer and your referees in preparing written references outlining your competence. You will want to brief them properly and for them to be accessible to potential employers.

What are your career goals over the next 3-5 years?

This is a popular question because logical and well-considered personal and career goals demonstrate your maturity and your commitment to your occupation or profession.

You can answer this question with confidence since you have already prepared your career plan and know what skills you wish to develop and how this translates in terms of job title and company and sector.

Your answer should be realistic, clear and succinct and ideally reveal some congruence between your career goal and where this position will lead you.

If this position doesn't fit naturally into your career plan, not only will you have difficulty in selling yourself as the ideal candidate but you should also consider the validity of either your career plan or this job application.

How would you describe your relationship with your current manager and how would they describe it?

You are likely to have at least one question on how you relate to people, particularly if the job involves contact with others. The interview itself will portray much of what the interviewer wants to know about your personal and social skills but you should be able to describe your relationship with your manager and contemporaries and, if relevant, your subordinates. If you do have an issue, then you need to provide a balanced rather than a one-sided assessment and remember that this question will be asked of your referees.

What did your latest performance appraisal highlight about you?

This is a good question and you should be able to discuss the contents critically. While you will want to portray the good points, you should also be prepared to discuss some of the issues that were raised, if any, and how you are overcoming or improving on these limitations. Most interviewers will also be asking this question of your referees so be careful about using your creative abilities.

What salary are you seeking in your next role?

Questions about your compensation are inevitable and indeed desirable. It's a process of negotiation and, naturally, you will want your salary to be as high as possible without impossible demands being attached. The employer will want your remuneration to be as low as possible without compromising your desire and commitment.

Therefore you need to communicate your desired salary range, perhaps using your current salary as a guide, and at the same time reinforce the reasons you believe you are worth that salary in terms of the value you can bring to the position and the company.

You want to make a strong statement without closing the door on your chances. This approach covers all bases.

There are different views on whether you should give a direct answer to this question until you know whether it's a job you are interested in and whether the employer is interested in you, as these two factors may change your answer.

Certainly an employer's propensity to reward you will depend on their desire to employ you which should increase through the selection process. My view is that from your research you will know your likely salary range in the market and this is the answer you should give. At the negotiation stage you are just trying to ensure you are near the top of that range.

Asking difficult questions

After you have answered questions about your experience, you usually have the opportunity to ask questions. This may be limited in the first interview where the employer perceives they are 'buying' but, as the selection process continues, they will begin to 'sell' more to you as a prospective employee.

Asking questions is important as it provides you with a greater insight into the organisation and the job itself, enabling you to make a more informed decision. You should ask a range of questions about those aspects of the job or the organisation that concern you most. Asking different interviewers the same question can be helpful because you obtain different perspectives and, if you ask good questions in the right way, you will come across as being thorough, analytical and professional. Delivery is as important as content and by asking open-ended and concise questions you will generate more useful information than simple yes-no questions.

You should listen attentively and ask follow-up questions where relevant. To help you structure your questions there are four main topics:

1. About the job itself
Assuming that you have a job description and/or the interviewer has described the job in some detail, you will want to ask questions that will give you more information about the key issues. Three possible questions are:

Why did the job come about? If it's an existing job why did the person move on or, if it's a new job, why has it been created?
What you are seeking here is clarity – whether the interviewer/manager really knows the reasons for the job and if their response is a logical one.

For example, if it's a new role you need to be convinced that the rationale for creating the position is sound and that you are going to have the support and resources required to do the job properly. If the job is a replacement job, why did the person move? It's a great sign if they were promoted to a new role in the same organisation, not so good if they moved on from the organisation, particularly after a short period of time. If they are still with the organisation, it may be worth asking if you could speak with them about the role. It's an unorthodox request but can provide you with another perspective on the role and the issues and challenges associated with it.

What are the key issues you need to resolve or work on in the first few weeks and months of the role?

Often the answer to this question will give you the essence of the job and will outline the immediate issues and challenges. If this is different from what has been described, you need to resolve the differences. If it's the same, it gives you some confidence that the role will be as described.

How will you assess that I'm doing a good job?
In understanding how your performance will be assessed, you had better understand the key issues of the job and what factors will be used to appraise your output. This is a reasonableness check for you. If you think that the job is too easy or too hard and the appraisal mechanism or resources available don't reflect this then this should affect your decision on the job or at least provide you with further questions.

How and where does this position fit into the structure of the department and do you have an organisational chart?
Sometimes jobs have titles that portray a certain level of responsibility. If you ask the interviewer to show you an organisational chart and describe just how the people in the department or division work together with a particular emphasis on your role, you will get a better idea of how you will fit in and whether it's a role you want.

2. About the organisation
In building your career it helps if you are with an organisation with a clear vision and good values and one that emphasises the importance of developing its people.

What is the organisation's vision and values?
If the organisation is large with a comprehensive website, you are likely to have researched this question prior to the interview. However it's still useful to ask, possibly with reference to the division you are interviewing with, about its vision and values. You can then deduce whether they correspond with your own.

I have noticed from my research that your organisation faces the challenge of 'xyz' in its key business sector. How will it

respond to that challenge?
Your research may have revealed that the organisation competes in a business niche or sector with specific challenges and issues, which may be positive or negative. By phrasing the question as above, you indicate that you have done some research and understand some of the issues but are interested to learn more, all good traits to display in an interview.

If I am successful in this role, what other opportunities would be open to me and do you have recent examples of people moving on within the organisation?
The nature and seniority of the role will determine the way you ask this question but essentially, you are trying to understand whether it's usual for the organisation to promote from within. You want to hear both reassuring words about the organisation's commitment to you and your career and have recent examples to back it up.

3. About your prospective line manager
Issues and conflicts with one's direct manager are one of the key reasons why people want to move jobs so it would be helpful to understand more about their pedigree and perspective on work.

Can you tell me about your background and how and why you joined this organisation?
This is a great question to ask. You want to learn about the pedigree of the person who is likely to be your mentor for the next phase of your career and from whom you will need to learn. Most managers are only too happy to talk about their background and you can often deduce all sorts of traits and qualities from their answer.

What do you perceive as your strengths and what are the qualities you do and don't like to see in your team members?
This is more of the same and is really three questions in one – you're asking them where they see their strengths which is obviously important for your ability to learn from them and to see

if there are any unexpected issues arising from the qualities response.

4. About the assignment process
What is the next step in the selection process from here and when should I expect to hear from you next?
This is obviously helpful to you in understanding the process and timelines involved which may be important with regard to other opportunities you are considering.

Finish in style

While first impressions are important, as both the interviewer and yourself form an instant judgment about each other, final impressions are also crucial in that you can sway a neutral view to positive with a strong, positive finish.

When the interviewer has signalled the end of the interview or you sense it's coming to an end, you should thank the interviewer for their time and reaffirm your interest in the position and in working with them (the individual and the organisation). If you have the opportunity, briefly (and it should be briefly) summarise why you would be good in the position and then determine the next stage in the process and when that will be. Ideally, you would have been able to shake their hand and establish good eye contact during your summary.

You should use this approach even if your initial reaction to the job is negative – it's always easier to change your mind from yes to no than from no to yes.

If you didn't receive a business card at the beginning of the interview then ensure you politely ask for one now. You will want to send them a follow-up email or letter and a business card will enable you to do this.

Video conference interviews

Increasingly, organisations are using technology within their selection process particularly in the early stages and for international assignments where video interviews are replacing phone interviews. Interviewing by video technology reduces the need for candidates to travel at predetermined times for face-to-face interviews which, in theory, increases the number of potential interview timeslots to choose from and shortens the selection timeline.

Although the way you prepare and perform for a video interview shouldn't differ from a face to face interview, you need to ensure you have a quiet room with a neutral backdrop where you won't be interrupted. You also have the challenge to project your personality in a video which is more difficult than face to face.

If in doubt prior to an important video interview, practise!

Follow up after the interview

Following up after the interview is just another branding opportunity for you. Always write a short letter or email to the interviewer thanking them for their time, reaffirming your interest in the position and why you think you would be good for the role. It's important to be specific and address their key needs and outline why you are the solution. Be confident but concise and articulate in your letter.

About 24 hours after the interview is the best time to send the letter, as you will appear to have 'slept' on the interview and be taking a considered view.

TAKE ACTION
1. Project a consistent and positive message no matter how many times you are interviewed for a position.

2. Aim to develop instant rapport with your interviewer by projecting energy, interest and sincerity and by mirroring your interviewer's style.

3. Work on your body language so you come across as confident and relaxed.

4. Preparation is key – rehearse how you will answer difficult questions and come up with some of your own to find out if it's really the job for you.

Chapter nine

Other selection criteria

Behaviour-based interviews are by far and away the most popular form of selection because they encompass both the presentation of facts and gut feel and answer the 'can you, will you and team' questions. However they are also hugely subjective based on who is asking the questions and interpreting the answers and, for that reason, many employers seek to complement the results of the interview with other selection methods. In your job search you need to prepare for these and consider the likely outcomes.

Résumé review and portal applications

Most organisations will use a review of the résumé to ensure it contains the key criteria that are required either via a personal and individual critique or by using technology to discard or reject résumés that don't possess certain required criteria (eg. educational or professional qualifications, language skills, visas and so on). If you know you don't have the required criteria but feel that overall you should still be considered, then you have to find ways of circumventing the technology used in the selection process. This is most likely achieved by finding a decision maker in the process and selling your skills and abilities to that person.

Psychometric tests

Psychometric, or personality, tests are very popular as an insight to an individual's personality and so are used extensively in internal learning and development and in external selection.

It is likely that you will have to take one sometime if you are seeking to progress to a senior executive position and I would thoroughly recommend you invest the time and money early in your career to take one.

A test such as Myers Briggs will help you greatly with your self-analysis as well as giving you practice in the test procedure.

Having called them 'tests' in the first paragraph, I should add that they are not really tests at all in that they do not have right or wrong answers. Psychometric or aptitude tests measure, among other things, a person's intelligence, personality or aptitude in a particular discipline and can help establish or confirm that person's competence for a particular job and whether their style and approach will fit the team or organisation. They are usually in the form of a number of questions, some of which are related and many of which appear unrelated. Depending on the combination of tests, it can take an hour or several hours to complete. The results are then interpreted and communicated by qualified practitioners.

There are hundreds of different types of tests but the most common focus on:

→ Verbal reasoning (which test how well you understand ideas expressed in words and how you think and reason with words)

→ Numerical reasoning (which test your understanding and reasoning with numbers)

→ Abstract reasoning (which test how good you are at thinking in abstract terms (ie. dealing with problems that are not presented in a numerical or verbal format).

Different organisations use different tests and look for different outcomes so it is difficult to revise or practise for a specific test. The best advice in taking a test is to be as alert and calm as you can be and ensure that you answer each question as truthfully and honestly as you can. As I mentioned above, I would recommend you take some well-known tests on your own account and this will give you valuable practice as well as useful information in your career management self-appraisal.

If you take several series of tests for different positions and the outcomes are not as you would wish, then there are books and courses which can help you to practise sample questions and tests.

Reference checking

Behaviour-based reference checks are a key part of the selection process. Most employers will want to verify the information you have provided through résumés, interviews and personality tests with external third parties. The job search etiquette is that they will seek your permission to discuss your application with two or three referees. The more credibility the referees have in the eyes of your potential employer, the more credence they will place on their answers.

Referees are an important part of your career management as well as your job search. Ideally, throughout your career you should nurture and develop relationships with work colleagues usually older and more experienced than yourself who you feel can become 'expert advisors' on your career. These are likely to be people with whom you have a rapport and whose advice on your career you would accept and value. Ask them if they are willing to mentor you and, if appropriate, become your referee for your job applications.

They don't need to be constant throughout your career and, indeed, as you develop it's important to have at least one referee who is or has been a manager or senior colleague and who can provide potential employers with information and comments about you that have some credence and authority.

Ideally, you should meet with each of your mentors or referees at least once a year to keep them appraised of your career progress and ask their advice and counsel. Before your job search commences, identify your potential referees and discuss your plans with them. They will be a useful sounding board and will help you formulate your message to the job market.

Discuss your interviews with them as they may also know the company and be able to add some special advice. Alert them to the possibility of being contacted and let them know the company and position you are being interviewed for so they can be prepared to answer on your behalf.

It is important that your referees answer the questions asked of them in the same way as you so you are both promoting the same message to potential employers. Any differences will detract from the strength of your message and the application itself.

Social events

As a recruiter, I recommend to our clients that they meet potential senior executives in a social situation as this creates a different selection dynamic. Often the candidates will let down their guard with a glass or two of wine under their belt. We suggest a formal dinner at a restaurant with the candidate and their partner (if they have one) and a few of the organisation's senior line managers and partners.

The occasion will be deemed a 'relaxed, social get together' but beware because it will be anything but. As a job seeker this is a difficult part of the job search process because much of the event – venue, seating plan and line of conversation – is out of your control.

If you have a steady partner then he or she is an important part of your job search team and should be aware of the role and organisation. It is likely that they will be asked an array of seemingly innocuous questions about your life together by the other partners and your advice to them has to be to stay calm and be themselves. They need to be supportive of you but neither aggressive nor defensive during the evening. Discuss beforehand the range of topics you both feel comfortable talking about, the range of answers you will give and the questions you can ask of the others. If either you or your partner feels uncomfortable about them being there, then make a plausible excuse for them not to go.

Finally, two further pieces of advice: don't drink alcohol or smoke and, secondly, use this event to your advantage. Be socially engaging, ask as many relevant questions as you can of your potential manager and their partner and be interested in their lives and family. If you can positively influence 'the partners' you will go a long way towards gaining approval.

Security clearances

For some specialist and senior roles, you will be subject to a security check either focused on your personal history and circumstances or fiduciary situation. There's nothing you can especially plan for here. If you do have a sizeable issue such as a fraud conviction while seeking a senior finance role, honesty is the best approach. Even though that will reduce the number of available opportunities, you will at least be in control of your application.

TAKE ACTION
1. Do a personality test for practice and self-analysis.

2. Build relationships with referees and make sure potential employers are receiving consistent messages about your brand.

3. Be on your guard at social events thinly disguised as job interviews – don't relax to the point that you jeopardise your chances.

Chapter ten

Common job search issues and solutions

There can be many reasons why your job search is faltering but the key ones are connected with getting from one stage of the job search process to the next and then finally a job offer you are happy with. The key stages are:

- Being sure what you want to do and of the message you are projecting to potential employers

- Creating sufficient interest in you through a well-constructed résumé and the various job search channels to obtain interviews with interested employers

- Creating sufficient interest in interviews to obtain a job offer

- Receiving an offer at a salary you would be happy with

- Obtaining two or more offers at a similar time to enable you to have greater choice of opportunities.

We explore these stages below.

Unsure of your next move?

If you are unsure of your next internal or external move, you are likely to be projecting an uncertain, confused image to potential employers. It's important to be sure of your next move before you start your job search.

Review your own strengths and weaknesses and discuss your circumstances with people who know you and can provide relevant advice. Then talk with your peers from school/university and other friends with similar backgrounds about their jobs, the organisations they work for and their likes and dislikes.

Surf the internet job sites to find job descriptions that interest you and the skills and abilities you need to obtain those jobs.

This will hopefully assist you in focusing on the next step.

Not winning interviews?

If you are not winning interviews it will be for one of four main reasons:

→ Your message isn't being communicated effectively through your résumé and application letter for the jobs and employers you are seeking.

→ The channels you are using to help find you a job (job advertisements, recruiters, direct approach, your network) aren't generating leads for interviews.

→ Your job search is spasmodic and poorly organised.

→ Employers are not recognising your skills and abilities for the jobs you are applying for.

Potential solutions are:

→ Critically review your résumé and application letter. Does it REALLY sell you and project the right qualities to potential employers?

→ Review your efforts with each job search channel. Are you building rapport in your approach? Are those people assisting you motivated to help you and will they project the right message to the right people? If not, you need to change your approach to ensure they are.

→ Ensure your job search is sufficiently intense and efficient to be able to produce a variety of opportunities. You need to be organised, positive and persistent.

→ Ensure that there is a good fit between the needs of potential employers when hiring and your skills and abilities. If there isn't, for whatever reason, you are unlikely to win interviews.

Finishing second in interviews

Or third. Or fourth. You need to finish first to win the offer and if you didn't, it's likely that in one or all of the following you weren't able to convince the potential employer that you were right for the job:

→ You don't have the skills and abilities to do the job.

→ You don't appear to want the role or it isn't a logical next step.

→ You and the interviewer don't have the necessary rapport.

The most likely reason is the third. If the hiring manager likes you, he/she is much more likely to hire you, so you must work hard on developing rapport during the selection process.

When there are too few opportunities

If you are only winning occasional interviews and offers, this may be due to poor job search technique (see above) or a lack of demand in the market for your portfolio of skills and abilities. You may need to re-analyse your approach and career plan with regard to what skills and abilities are in demand by employers. The internet job sites are again useful research tools for this review.

What to do if you are offered too low a salary

You may have an over-inflated opinion of your worth but this is unlikely if you have thoroughly researched the market and its value of your skills and abilities. It's more likely that your potential employer is consciously, or unconsciously, downgrading your value because either:

→ They believe the supply and demand factors are sufficiently in their favour to enable them to reduce the market rate salary for this position, or

→ You haven't been able to communicate sufficiently well the unique nature of your skills and abilities and how you will be able to provide solutions to their issues and challenges.

In attempting to improve your starting remuneration package, you do need to discuss, ideally with the hiring manager, the constraints in place and the rationale for you wanting to achieve a higher remuneration package. In doing this you MUST first create the right environment for a discussion, namely that you are very positive about the organisation and the opportunity but, as the salary offered is lower than expected, you want to discuss this further to see if there is any room for negotiation.

You need to be able to re-affirm your skills and abilities and how relevant they are to the position and see if there is scope for improving the starting salary or related benefits. If not, then try and obtain a performance-based review six months after starting your new role.

If your campaign isn't working

If after three to four months of a serious job search you are not making progress and are not winning interviews, you need to undergo a serious review of your job search campaign. Summon external help and invite those close to your search, including your referees, to give you assistance. A supportive but critical external review may shed light on why you're not making progress. Review, regroup and double your efforts.

TAKE ACTION
1. If you are offered a salary that is too low and there doesn't seem to be room for negotiations, consider asking for a performance-based pay review in 3-6 months.

2. If your job search campaign is proving fruitless, objectively reassess your goals and strategies and get help doing so if you need to.

Chapter eleven

Is it the job for you?

Once you have received a job offer, you don't have much time to decide on whether or not it's right for you and whether you should accept or decline. The organisation making the offer will usually want a decision within a few days as they have a position to fill and will want to keep their selection process moving to a successful conclusion. However there are several important stages.

Analyse the job in relation to your plan

One of the benefits of having a well-defined career and job search plan is that it's easier to assess whether the job you are seeking is the right one for you.

It's likely that you would have responded to a job advertisement or position description that was attractive, although sometimes you are given the opportunity to interview with an organisation without really knowing about the job in hand. Either way, the interview process will enable you to decide and your analysis of the opportunity should be something like this:

The job itself

→ Can I use my existing knowledge, skills and experience to manage the responsibilities of the role?

→ Are there aspects of the role that are new to me and which will extend me and my range of knowledge, skills and experience?

→ By undertaking this job will my skill base remain marketable and will my career continue in the direction I want it to go?

→ Does the job excite me?

→ Do I want to do it?

The individual manager
→ Is this a person I can work with?
→ Is this a person I can learn from?
→ Do I respect their style and values?
→ Do I like them?

The organisation itself
→ Do I believe in their vision?
→ Do I trust their values?
→ Do I like the people I have met?
→ Is it financially secure?
→ Can it offer me career progression?
→ Is it growing and in a growth sector?

Practical aspects
→ Am I happy with the hours I need to work?
→ Am I happy with the working conditions?
→ Can I get to and from work relatively quickly and safely?

There may be other questions you wish to ask yourself when making the decision but the above would cover most considerations. You would want to answer most, if not all, the questions affirmatively and where you don't, this is a sign that the job is not right for you.

Sometimes you will be presented with opportunities that you are excited by and interested in but which won't develop your career as per your career plan. You then have one of two choices: reject the job and stick with your career plan or accept the job and change your career plan. Either alternative is acceptable but you should just be aware of the choices you have to make.

You really want to be close to deciding on the role prior to what you think is your final interview so that you can make a quick decision or fine tune the conditions of the offer. This is your ideal scenario even if sometimes it doesn't happen that way.

It's also useful to discuss your options with your referees and close family and friends. Although it always remains your decision, they may highlight some interesting perspectives.

Negotiate to make it attractive

One question missing from the above analysis was the question of compensation and benefits.

Once you have decided the opportunity is good for you and your career you need to assess what salary and benefits package fairly compensates you and is in line with the market. Decide what components of the package (base salary, benefits, short-term incentives such as bonuses, long-term incentives) are essential to you and what you can do without.

There is no common rule to where organisations pitch their offers. Some will go low and expect to have to negotiate while others will set a 'fair rate of pay' immediately and not be open to negotiation.

The more unique you are and the closer you fit to the desired profile, the more likely it will be that organisations will be prepared to negotiate higher or will set their offer high. If they have several people of equal ability and fit available to do the job then they are less likely to be negotiable. You have to weigh up a number of factors:

→ Your situation. How much do you want this role? How many other potential offers do you have? What do you think is a fair market rate?

→ The market. What are the market rate pressures? In the current market the pressures are almost all downward.

→ The organisation. Have they given anything away throughout the process about their intentions, their feelings towards you, other candidates? Do you think you are their first choice? Their only choice?

Ideally they are likely to make you a verbal offer, which will give you a benchmark. Alternatively, they may offer you the job subject to agreeing on a satisfactory package and expect to negotiate from there. Either way your approach should be as follows:

→ Try to negotiate salary with your hiring manager, as they will be more involved and more likely to be able to authorise an increase. This isn't always possible, however, particularly in large organisations where HR policy sometimes dictates otherwise.

→ Confirm that you want the job and why you want the job. In this way you continue to build rapport between yourself and your hiring manager. Explain up front that you are seeking more and the reasons for this. Negotiate one point at a time, beginning with base, then benefits and then bonus.

→ If the employer can't or won't move on the offer, then try to introduce a performance-related component such as a salary review after three or six months, a performance bonus or additional leave if certain targets are met.

→ Be prepared to back off or not discuss issues that are not important to you or where you have already gained some buy-in from the employer. They have to feel that the negotiation isn't all one way.

→ At the end of your discussion, either reaffirm your interest and ask for the offer in writing or, if you are certain the offer does not match your expectations, thank the executive very much for their time but explain that you cannot accept the role at that level of compensation.

Once you have received the offer in writing, compare the terms with your understanding of the verbal offer and, assuming all is in order, then write back confirming your acceptance. In most cases this will be your only form of written confirmation until you start when you will receive a full contract of employment.

Decline with dignity

While you should turn the job offer down if you feel it's not right for you, this should be done professionally. If you feel sufficiently confident, you should phone the hiring manager and (broadly) explain your reasons but, even if you don't call, then send a letter to those people who met you thanking them for their time and interest.

This is an investment in your future. That organisation or that hiring manager may at some time be recruiting for your 'dream job' and if you have acted professionally you will have an advantage over your competitors. You will at least be likely to win an interview. Even without the letter, you might but with the letter it will be almost guaranteed.

Resigning and dealing with counter offers

Usually the hardest part about accepting a new job is resigning from your old one.

You may feel uncomfortable in resigning because of your loyalty towards your present organisation and, quite possibly, because you may have friendships with your colleagues and your manager that could be tested by your move.

However you have thought through the move carefully and shouldn't be diverted from your course of action.

You should request a private face to face meeting with your manager and announce your decision to resign. You should ensure you deliver this 'unpleasant' message in a friendly, courteous manner explaining that although you have enjoyed working together, an exciting opportunity has arisen that you believe can advance your career.

Emphasise that your decision to leave was made carefully and does not reflect any negative feelings you have toward the organisation or the staff.

Finally, thank your manager for the opportunity you have been given by the organisation and assure them that you will do everything you can to make your departure as smooth and painless as possible.

This may not be strictly the case but your manager could well end up being a referee and therefore you want to ensure that they remain positive about you. Being antagonistic and vengeful will do nothing to help your cause.

It is likely that your manager will want to discuss the reasons for resignation in some detail to both better understand your rationale so they can learn from the situation and also potentially with a view to changing your mind.

Should you be drawn into a conversation, ensure that you stay calm and objective. Being emotional cannot be in your best interests.

Either at the meeting or soon afterwards, follow up with a resignation letter that should be short, simple and to the point.

Usually your manager will accept your resignation with disappointment and regret but will be prepared to wish you well as an individual. Occasionally it becomes acrimonious, particularly if your manager feels the situation is sensitive or embarrassing to them as an individual.

Depending on the circumstances, your manager may make you a counter offer to entice you to stay. The counter offer may be a financial inducement, an increase in responsibility or an alternative career option.

While in most cases it's a short-term attempt to prevent losing a valued employee, sometimes it's also a genuine attempt to redress a lack of foresight or poor timing.

Your manager could use a variety of approaches to try and convince you that leaving would be a mistake including flattery, shock, anger or trying to plant doubt in your mind about your potential employer. They may also involve others in the process.

Whatever the counter-offer approach, it's likely to involve a plan of how things can be different and often a promise of a higher salary.

Whether or not you accept the counter offer depends on your own career plan, the logic and fit of the original offer and how strong the emotional ties to your current employer are.

There are dangers attached to accepting counter offers such as a potential question mark regarding your loyalty which could affect further career advancement and/or job security and the possibility that things stay exactly the same for three or four months by which time your alternative job opportunity will have gone.

It is important to remind yourself of your original reasons for deciding to resign. If they remain valid, you should proceed with your resignation and decline the counter offer preferably immediately and decisively but courteously.

A persistent employer may try several times but will eventually give up if you maintain your resolve.

Depart professionally

With emotions on both sides potentially running high during the resignation process, there are sometimes opportunities for things to be said and done that are later regretted. Always strive to depart the organisation professionally. You may be required to finish immediately or indeed work your full notice or somewhere in between.

Whatever the circumstances, by maintaining your dignity and integrity you will be highly thought of which is an investment in your current and future reputation.

TAKE ACTION

1. Before accepting a job, assess if it's really the smartest next step for you.

2. Resign from your existing position with professionalism at all costs.

3. If your existing employer makes a counter offer, remind yourself why you wanted to leave in the first place.

Chapter twelve

Make the best start to your new job

Prepare to succeed

You have done the hard part in securing the job at an appropriate salary whether through an internal move or an external selection process. You should now maximise your chances of making it a successful move by preparing for your new job in the same way you did your interviews.

If it's a permanent role, you should ideally try to take some time off between the end of your old job and the beginning of your new job in order to rest and start to focus on the challenge ahead. It's also unlikely that you will be taking a holiday within the first six to nine months of your new role, so a break will help you re-energise. Two weeks is ideal and a week probably the minimum required.

If you have secured a contract, especially a short-term contract, it's likely they will want you to start immediately so you will need to complete your preparation on a weekend.

Before you start your new job, email or write to your network with the news, personally thanking those people who assisted you with your search. This is common sense as well as common courtesy because you may need those people to help you again in the future and they won't be inclined to do so if you haven't notified or thanked them this time.

Review your job specification and think about where you need to focus your energies in the critical first weeks and months of your new role. If it's a senior role where you need to impact quickly and decisively, you may want to discuss your likely approach with your manager off site prior to starting.

Ensure that you visit your doctor, dentist, hairdresser and any other personal service contacts before you start. The last thing you want is to be absent from work due to circumstances that could have been foreseen.

Review your personal diary and plan to cut back on outside commitments for the first few months. You need to focus all you can on the job in hand.

Plan your wardrobe for your first week and, if necessary, buy some new work clothes to help you make a positive impression.

Week one – create a favourable impression

Your first day and week is all about creating a favourable impression among your colleagues and managers. You will be the focus of everyone's comments and critiques from the way you walk to how you engage in conversation and people will quickly form a positive, neutral or negative impression of you. This is particularly so if you are in a supervisory, management or leadership position.

Although settling into a work pattern quickly is important, you won't be judged on your productivity as much as your relationships in week one. Your approach should be to focus on:

→ Projecting a friendly, positive approach with everyone you meet (without being sycophantic), even if they don't reciprocate

→ Learning the names of the people you need to know from your immediate colleagues and your manager as well as the receptionist and security manager. Ask your manager for an organisational chart (and ideally a seating plan) with names on to assist you

→ Ensuring you learn the telephone and basic technology systems. They may appear elementary but if you have to ask more than a few times how to make an outside call, your credibility starts to falter

→ Trying to build the foundations of good working relationships with the important people in your working life. This involves good social skills

→ Listening and learning. Be a sponge to your environment and what is going on

→ Meet with your manager to reaffirm again the boundaries of your role, the key issues and suggested emphasis and any likely problem areas you should be aware of

→ Similarly, meet briefly with your relevant co-workers to understand how they like to work, what they perceive the issues and challenges to be as well as any problem areas you should be aware of

→ Obtain a copy of your contract of employment and read it carefully at home. In senior positions, it's advisable to obtain a draft contract before you resign as the contract could contain clauses that are unacceptable to you. However, for most other positions you will receive it in week one. If you are not used to reading such contracts ask one of your referees to review it with you. If you have additional concerns, seek the advice of an employment lawyer and certainly look to have the matter addressed quickly by your employer.

Month one – focus on relationships and productivity

Once your first week is over, you must begin to focus on building your key internal and external relationships and raising your productivity to an initial acceptable level. In particular:

→ Introduce yourself to everyone in your office or division that you didn't meet in your first week, even if you are not going to be working directly with them. Being positive and open will begin to build a positive groundswell of opinion for you within the office.

→ If you are managing a team, call a meeting of that team and outline your basic philosophies. It's far too early to be outlining visions and plans (unless of course you have been promoted internally in which case you may know the issues and be confident of your approach). Explain that you will meet everyone individually in the near future and then follow up on that promise.

→ Get to grips with the basics of your job quickly. Read all the available documentation, including your budgets, and listen and learn. You shouldn't make big or sweeping changes. Take time to learn the system, the people and the culture.

→ Make yourself productive immediately. Do things that are easy and safe but which generate value for the organisation and your internal reputation.

Your first three months – learn to understand the culture

During your first three months you must continue to raise your productivity and develop good relationships but also work hard on learning to understand the culture. Your eventual success in the organisation will depend on the congruence between your own values and standards and those of the organisation. If they are closely aligned, you are likely to feel comfortable and confident. If they aren't, there are likely to be situations in which you feel distinctly uncomfortable and personality conflicts could ensue.

Listen, learn and observe how the company operates and build your internal credibility before acting in defiance of the culture. Of course, it's a balance – while you can be individual and creative, you don't want to challenge or threaten the status quo straight away (unless of course you have been specifically hired to do so).

After three months – build your profile and performance

After three months you should review your own performance and discuss your progress with your manager.

You need to know if you are on the right track or at odds with the organisation. From this point on, you are striving for optimum performance in your relationships and your work.

> **TAKE ACTION**
> 1. Take a break to re-energise before starting a new job if you can.
>
> 2. Focus on first impressions and building relationships in your new workplace before making sweeping changes.

The Paul Lyons 'Win' Series ...

This exciting and highly resourceful series of books is written by *the* expert in the field of careers and recruitment. With twenty five years of expertise backing the principles and advice on every page, this series is an insider's perspective on the recruitment process that should be on every job-seeker, employee, and employer's bookshelf.

Win That Interview

Win That Interview helps job seekers develop the preparation and planning skills that are a crucial foundation for an impressive and successful interview. As a careers and recruitment expert, Paul Lyons brings to *Win That Interview* years of experience in interviewing candidates, providing job-applicants with a thorough and informed idea of what recruiters are looking for and how to be selected as the ideal candidate. This valuable guide explains and sets the standards for all aspects of performing well in an interview. It also includes hundreds of relevant interview questions that an employer or recruiter may ask, and how you should answer them for the best chance of success.

Win That Star Employee

Win that Star Employee is designed to help hiring managers recruit the best candidates for their team. Author and experienced recruiter, Paul Lyons, uses his years of experience in candidate sourcing and selection to provide employers with an excellent guide to defining the requirements of their ideal 'star employee', and then, how to attract, select, recruit, retain and nurture that star employee. With solid advice on creating an irresistible and inspiring dream team culture that no star employee will want to leave, and handy tips on how to effectively source and interview candidates, this is a vital tool for anyone who is responsible for hiring high performing individuals.